Lifeworth

Lifeworth

Finding Fulfillment
Beyond Networth

DANA J. COUILLARD
& HAL D. COUILLARD

Kingsley
PUBLISHING

Additional copies of *Lifeworth: Finding Fulfillment Beyond Networth* for
clients, employees, family, or friends can be ordered directly from
www.lifeworth.ca. Contact us for information on quantity discounts.

Contact Lifeworth Inc. for information on author interviews or speaking
engagements, www.lifeworth.ca

Published in Canada and the United States by Kingsley Publishing, 2012
www.kingsleypublishing.ca

Kingsley
PUBLISHING

Cover and interior design: Dean Pickup
Front cover image: © Chris Knorr/Design Pics/Corbis
Author photos: Rob Olson Photography

Printed in Canada by Friesens

2012/1
First Edition

Library and Archives Canada Cataloguing in Publication

Couillard, Dana, 1951–
    Lifeworth : finding fulfillment beyond networth / Dana
Couillard and Hal Couillard.

Includes bibliographical references.
ISBN 978-1-926832-08-1

    1. Quality of life. 2. Well-being.
I. Couillard, Hal, 1953– II. Title.

HN25.C68 2011   306   C2011-905660-7

This book is dedicated to the memory
of our youngest brother, Stuart.

"We'll see you down the road."

Your brothers, Dana, Hal, and Craig

CONTENTS

ACKNOWLEDGEMENTS

We set out on a journey to create a *Lifeworth* experience by writing this book together. It has been a challenging and rewarding trip, but we have not made the trip alone. We would like to thank the many people who have contributed to the completion of this journey.

The individual stories that we collected from across Canada are an integral part of this book: John Davidson, Martha Birkett, Paul Henderson, Katy Hutchison, Alan Hobson, Lindsay Sears, Tom Droog, Jeanelle Mitchell, Susan Wetmore, and Dawn Straka. Your patience during the interview process and in reviewing your chapters is much appreciated. Your stories give the book many different perspectives for others to build on.

Charlene Dobmeier, our publisher and mentor, kept us focused and moving forward. Working with the two of us has probably been a little like trying to rope cats and herd snakes, neither of which is easy! Your patience, professionalism, and editorial perspective in bringing this book to completion has been awesome and is much appreciated!

Alex Frazer-Harrison, our editor, challenged us with his questions, comments, and suggestions, helping us see our book with new eyes. Just when we thought we had something to work with, you helped us to recognize that writing is a building and polishing process. Wax on, wax off; wax on, wax off. Thanks for helping us through that process.

As he created the first few drafts of the book cover, Dean Pickup, our graphic artist, listened to our comments and then blew us away with the cover you see now. Dean, your work was integral to achieving the look and feel of the book.

Lyn Cadence, our PR consultant, provided much-needed guidance to two later-in-life writers who felt somewhat overwhelmed with the opportunities available using social media to let people know about our book. Your professional experience in promoting the book through more traditional channels was also a learning experience for us.

A big thanks to Nick Pszeniczny, Executive Vice President, Individual Distribution and Marketing, Great West Life/London Life/Canada Life; Mike Cunneen, Senior Vice President, Freedom 55 Financial and the Wealth and Estate Planning Group; Mike Rigato, Vice President and Chief Distribution Officer, Wealth and Estate Planning Group; Hugh Moncreiff, Senior Vice President, Great West Life; and Phil Marsillo, Senior Vice President, Canada Life. Your belief in and support for our project from the very start has been awesome.

Bob Schulz, faculty member of Haskayne School of Business at the University of Calgary, encouraged our early efforts to go forward and challenged us to expand the scope and reach of the book.

Dave Brown created the Lifeworth.ca website and continues to keep it functional for us.

For the past two years, *Lifeworth* has permeated our family conversations probably more often than we know. Our grown children, all professionals in their own right, helped to provide an intergenerational perspective for the book that we couldn't have accomplished without them.

We have saved the final thank you for the two most important people in our lives: our lifelong spouses and best friends, Penny (Hal) and Brenda (Dana). You read the chapters many times, supported us when it seemed we couldn't get unstuck, listened to our ideas and frustrations, supported the hours we took away from family and business for the book, and loved us even when we were grumpy! Thank you doesn't begin to cover it! ■

INTRODUCTION

Gross national product measures everything, in short,
except that which makes life worthwhile.

ROBERT F. KENNEDY

The concept of *Lifeworth* grew out of our discussions—as two brothers in our late-fifties—about purpose and meaning in our lives. Over the past few years, we have been talking about and trying to discover what the next phase of our lives would look like. Our children have graduated from school and are successfully making their way in their own worlds. We were both wondering, to differing degrees and in different ways, about the difference between "networth" and the worth of life.

Like most baby boomers, we were approaching a transition point in our lives, the transition into the second half, third quarter, or seventh inning (depending upon your sports metaphor of choice). We began to experience "the Clock." The Clock is the ever-present clock of time, the life clock, the clock over which we have no control—the clock our youth had allowed us to overlook for so many years. But, unlike most sports

1

clocks, this clock has no stop-time function! At some unknown point, the ticking of the life clock began to echo ever so slightly in the background of our thoughts. We came face to face with our own limitations and our own mortality. We began to experience a desire to live our lives more fully and to make a difference in the lives of others, more so than we had to this point. We began to ask:

- "Is this all there is?"

- "Is there more to life than money and networth?"

- "Am I living the life I want to live, and is it a worthwhile life?"

- "How will I be remembered when I am gone? What legacy will I leave?"

- "Will I have left my world a better place?"

We had watched with interest the transformation of Jack Nicholson's character, Warren Schmidt, in the film *About Schmidt* as he began to ask himself these same questions. We enjoyed belly laughs, not without some sense of irony, at the accomplishments of Edward Cole and Carter Chambers in *The Bucket List* (played, respectively, by Nicholson and Morgan Freeman). The "bucket list" concept came up often in our conversations. We realized that many of the items on Edward and Carter's bucket lists were peak experiences they wanted to have in their lives. We talked about some of the things we wanted to do, while we still had our physical and mental health.

We knew we weren't the only baby boomers experiencing this type of psychological and emotional transition. In everyone's life, there is a transition from a focus on networth to a focus on the worth of life, from focusing on accumulating wealth, resources, and material things to focusing on other people. All individuals will eventually arrive at this life-changing transition point—the only variable is *when*. It is a time when we begin to understand what is "enough" in terms of material comforts, a time to start experiencing our lives to the fullest, or to begin making a difference in the lives of others. Not everyone has equal resources, but all individuals have the opportunity to make some type of transition from "networth" to "lifeworth"—if they choose to do so.

Like most boomers, we had been focused on developing our careers, raising our families, and planning for our far-distant retirement. In our careers as a financial planner (Hal) and as a behavioural coach and educator to business owners, senior leaders, and professionals (Dana), the concept of networth often formed some part of client discussions. Networth has driven all of our lives for various reasons and to varying degrees. At some point that neither of us can remember (maybe age-related?), the word "lifeworth" presented itself as something different from, and beyond, networth.

Over time, we arrived at a working definition of *Lifeworth* that we felt best defined what we were looking for. We defined *Lifeworth* in terms of specific types of experiences. A *Lifeworth* experience is a peak experience that rockets us out of our Comfort Zone (more on Comfort Zones in Chapter 3). These peak experiences take us briefly into something we call the Lifeworth Zone (more on that zone in Chapter 5). They can also be about achieving certain challenges or growth in our lives. Or they can be about helping others meet their needs or achieve a peak experience.

Not all peak experiences are happy or positive, as you will discover in some of the stories in this book. Sometimes a peak experience is thrust into our lives with little or no warning: the death of a loved one, an unexpected job loss, a sudden heart attack or stroke—the list is a long one. However, we agreed that all peak experiences—positive or negative, planned or unexpected—are defining moments that alter how we view life as we move forward from the experience. They are experiences that present opportunities for growth, if we only take the time to pursue each opportunity as it presents itself. Peak experiences are those that take us out of the Comfort Zone that has been partly defined by our existing networth.

Out of the many resources available to us, we have identified three that are necessary in order to achieve most peak experiences: Time, Talent, and Treasure. We refer to these resources as the "Three Ts." All of us have them, to varying degrees.

Time is the amount of time we have available to us each day, and how effectively we use that resource. *Talent* is our innate ability to do certain things extremely well—things that we are passionate about, that energize us, that give us gratification. *Treasure* refers to the financial resources we have built up and have available at any given point in our lives. Giving to others can mean giving one or more of these Ts in a significant, sustainable, and meaningful way to make the world a better place.

Initially, we identified two types of peak experiences, which we saw as different ways of achieving a sense of *Lifeworth* in separate, somewhat distinct areas of life. One was doing things in our own lives to meet our own challenges and growing beyond our Comfort Zone. The other was doing things for others that took us out of our Comfort Zone. However, as we began to interview individuals for this book, we realized that the two areas could overlap. Sometimes both types of peak experiences are combined in one experience. In other cases, one type of experience can lead to the other.

At this point in our lives, neither of us was too sure we wanted to follow the lead of the stars of *The Bucket List* and jump out of an airplane, especially in tandem. We're close, but not that close! But we did decide to create a *Lifeworth* experience that we could share as brothers. Over a glass of wine (okay, maybe more than one), we decided to write a book about what was initially a somewhat-vague *Lifeworth* concept. And, if we could sell enough copies, we planned to donate a significant amount of the proceeds to organizations and causes important to us.

Through the struggle and frustration of trying to differentiate our book from the excellent work that already exists out there, without losing our purpose for it, we came to the conclusion that we did not want to create another self-help book for achieving purpose and meaning in one's life. Many fine books currently exist with well-thought-out steps, strategies, and tips for achieving a life worth living. For example, we were both familiar with the outstanding work of Frederic Hudson of the Hudson Institute in Santa Barbara, California. His book, *Life Launch: A Passionate Guide to the Rest of Your Life,* helps individuals find meaning and passion in their lives while understanding the life cycles they journey through over time. We had both read the excellent books written by Richard Lieder and David Shapiro: *Repacking Your Bags, Claiming Your Place at the Fire,* and *The Power of Purpose.* We had read William Bridges' works, *Transitions* and *The Way of Transitions,* and Max Lucado's *The Cure for the Common Life.* And there are many more great titles available in this area.

In most instances, there is no scarcity of information on how to do something. More likely, there is a lack of execution on our own part in actually doing it. Throughout history, stories have been, and continue to be, a powerful tool to pass learning and culture on to future generations. Stories resonate with us; we can identify with the storyteller. Stories help us act on things that are important to us. Through the stories of others, we can feel encouraged that others have made this journey before us. We begin to feel empowered to start our own journey.

We decided to explore the stories of people who have made the transition from networth to *Lifeworth* as a means of encouraging both others and ourselves to move into that area of our lives before it was too late— before our health or resources became potential barriers. We defined two distinct, yet inseparable, goals:

- To collect stories from both high-achievers and everyday people who are making, or have made, at least one transition from focusing on net-worth to focusing on *Lifeworth*.

- To create a reflective pool of stories in which every individual can locate possibilities for achieving a *Lifeworth* experience, on their terms and within reach of their abilities and resources.

We want to acknowledge that many, if not all, of us live lives worth living, even if we don't realize it. We do not want any confusion on that point. We contribute to our lives, to our families, and to society in the various ways that are available to us at that time. This is a good thing, something most of us strive for at our own levels of income, and for the life we have chosen to lead at that point. However, many of us can get trapped in different Comfort Zones throughout our lives.

The Comfort Zone can create complacency, a reduced sense of striving to discover and live our life's purpose, even a sense of boredom or rest-lessness. As you will read in Chapter 5, we have described a new zone con-nected to, but beyond, the Comfort Zone. We have called it the Lifeworth Zone. The focus of this book is to help individuals discover ways to test the waters of the Lifeworth Zone and to discover how to make periodic transitions from the Comfort Zone to the Lifeworth Zone over the course of their lives. When we talk about making the transition from networth to *Lifeworth*, we are talking about making leaps out of the Comfort Zone that our current resources have helped us to achieve and maintain.

Many of the individuals interviewed for this book were introduced to us personally by successful financial security advisors from across Canada, who, in turn, were associated with a variety of organizations, including Great-West Life, Canada Life, and London Life and its finan-cial security advice and planning divisions, Freedom 55 Financial and the Wealth and Estate Planning Group.

Why the financial planning sector? There are three reasons, actually. The first is that Hal has spent the past thirty-six years developing a successful career and practice in the financial planning sector. His network of peers across Canada was a ready source of referrals to clients who might be featured in this book. Second, for the past four years, Dana has had the good fortune to develop coaching relationships with a small group of successful financial planners. As he worked with these insightful entrepreneurs, he developed a better understanding of the tools and processes they use with their clients, and he wanted to explore this area in more depth. This leads to the third reason: most successful financial planners help their clients do more than create financial plans to accumulate networth over the course of their lives. Most go beyond this stage to help their clients identify opportunities to utilize their networth in many different and meaningful ways. They take their clients through various discovery processes to help them identify their core needs, strengths, motivators, and personal growth opportunities. Many of them also provide their clients with access to different resources that might be of benefit to them: books, DVDs, seminars, workshops, and presentations, to name only a few. It seemed like a natural and comfortable fit to draw out the stories of some of their clients in the area of *Lifeworth*.

In addition to referrals from financial planners, people already being interviewed for the book suggested others. This was an unexpected and pleasant twist in the process of gathering material. Everyone seemed to know someone who had a story to tell that might fit with the themes of the book.

The response was overwhelming and, at times, a bit unsettling—how could we fit them all in? We decided to create a few guidelines to help us select individuals who shared most or all of the following characteristics:

- Were generally in the midlife age or beyond.

- Had numerous personal and career accomplishments, and/or were generally happy with themselves and their life experiences.

- Had a sense of what is "enough" for themselves in terms of physical comforts—their physical needs had been met well enough, or maybe even abundantly, and they were now deriving satisfaction more from personal involvements and experiences than from material goods.

- Were known by friends and colleagues to have a true spirit of generosity, and were not strangers to taking on big challenges.

- Had a genuine sense of service and contribution, and were expressing those qualities by actively and consciously creating their own legacy, directly or indirectly.

- Had a strong sense of gratitude and appreciation and were giving back to the world in a significant, sustainable, and meaningful way.

- Had a desire to know that, in some small or large way, the world is a better place for their having been there.

At least, these are the guidelines we started with! We quickly learned that, for every guideline, there was an exception waiting to ambush us. And what rewarding exceptions they were! For example, we had the opportunity to interview Lindsay Sears, a world barrel-racing champion in her late twenties—definitely an exception to the "midlife age or beyond" guideline. What she has accomplished, and the difference she made in the lives of others at a "young" age (at least from our perspective), can only be described as remarkable.

To create some degree of consistency in collecting the stories, each interviewee was asked the following questions:

1. What created your desire to focus on creating and living a life worth living for yourself and/or for others?

2. Describe a peak experience in your life, if any, and what impact this experience has had on your life.

3. Describe a philanthropic experience in your life, if any, and what impact this experience has had on your life.

4. What would be your personal definition of *Lifeworth* or a life worth living?

5. What do you think your purpose is in your life?

6. If you died tomorrow, what types of legacies will you have left? How will you be remembered?

7. What suggestions or recommendations would you give to others who have not yet made, or perhaps are considering making, a transition to a peak experience in their lives?

The interviews were very free flowing, allowing each individual to express their creativity and tell their story. The questions were designed simply as placeholders to ensure that, somewhere during the conversation, we could gather most of the information we were looking for from each person.

Interviewees received an interview package that contained an overview of the book, a brief explanation of the terms "peak experience" and *Lifeworth*, and the interview questions. The interviews were recorded, transcribed, and reviewed for where they would best fit into the book. Each interviewee had input on how their stories appeared in the book; we wanted their stories to truly represent them.

Our first interview was with Paul Henderson, a Canadian sports icon from his years with the Toronto Maple Leafs and especially for scoring "*the* goal" for Team Canada in 1972. We didn't know what to expect—two relatively unknown guys living at the edge of the Rockies in Alberta, halfway across the country, talking with one of the hockey legends from our youth. It turned out to be an outstanding interview—actually more of a personal dialogue—with lots of bantering, give-and-take, and tremendous insight. We thought, "Wow, how will we be able to top that one?"

Then we interviewed Martha Birkett, a grandmother who rode her horse from Ottawa to Calgary in all kinds of true-Canadian weather over a period of four months to raise money and awareness for the Children's Wish Foundation. She riveted us to the telephone with her story of what she went through with her family—before the ride was even conceived! This was followed by an interview with John Davidson, who, with his son Jesse, started Jesse's Journey. This was the captivating story of a father and son on a mission to raise awareness of Duchenne muscular dystrophy, the condition from which Jesse suffered. Their goal was also to raise enough money to support research across North America to search for a cure for this debilitating and life-ending disease.

These were an awesome start to our interviews, and the journey continued with one inspiring personal story after another. With each interview, the momentum and the passion of the stories just kept building right up to the last interview with Alan Hobson, a Mount Everest summiteer, cancer survivor, and dedicated motivational speaker. He took us from the peaks of the mountains to the valleys of being diagnosed with cancer and back to the peaks of being a passionate speaker about surviving cancer. We are thankful to all of those inspired individuals who shared their stories with us as we worked at creating our own *Lifeworth* experience!

Lifeworth: Finding Fulfillment Beyond Networth was written to provide readers with new information and insight in the area of human dynamics—the underlying processes that lead to different motivators and behaviours in various situations throughout our lives. It was also written to provide readers with inspiration through the eyes of the individuals in this book, and through the peak experiences they have encountered. This journey is unique to each of them, and each has developed his or her own strategies aligned with his or her personality, motivations, core values, and resources. ■

SO NOW WHAT?

As the information, insight, and inspiring stories we collected over two years began to take shape in the first few chapters, we asked ourselves an introspective and slightly irreverent question: "So what? How does this apply to the reader? How can people use this information to create their own peak experiences and create their own sense of *Lifeworth*?"

We decided we would pose the same question to you, the reader, as points to reflect on or as challenges to take action. At the end of each story, we have added a brief section called "So Now What?" These sections give you an opportunity to reflect on the material in the chapter and to ponder how some small part of that story could affect or challenge you. Remember, one of our two goals was to create a reflective pool of brief stories in which every individual can locate possibilities for creating peak experiences for a *Lifeworth* experience, on their terms and within the reach of their abilities and resources.

We hope as you read and reflect on these stories, as well as on some of our own life experiences, however humble in comparison, the information and insight provided here will inspire you to take action in your own life.

Dana and Hal Couillard

CHAPTER ONE

LOSING YOUR
MARBLES

I want to be all used up when I die.

GEORGE BERNARD SHAW

W e don't know if you ever played marbles when you were a kid. But as little boys growing up on the prairies, playing marbles was a great pastime. It was fun, competitive, and, in a way, it helped to subconsciously shape our adult lives. We don't see the game being played much anymore. This simple, inexpensive game seems to have been replaced by expensive, fancy electronic ones, often encouraging time alone with very little human interaction.

For those of you who don't know the fabulous game of marbles, there are actually a number of different games to play. Here is one version: Any number of kids prepare the "game board" by digging four coffee cup-sized holes in the dirt at the corners of an imaginary square, with a fifth hole in the middle of the square. Each kid takes out a marble from a coveted bag of marbles and starts at the first hole that has been agreed upon by the group. After deciding who will go first, players cradle the marble in their first finger, held in place by the thumb, ready to "flick" the marble toward the first hole. The kids take turns "knuckling down" to shoot their marble at the next hole, or at someone else's marble. What skill, technique, and eyeballing of the lay of the land went into those shots! We became eagle-eyed hunters, scanning the game board for any slight dips or humps in the dusty ground, a tiny pebble, or a dry leaf that might deflect our marble from its target.

Figure 1.1

If you are fortunate enough to get your marble into the hole, you keep flicking to the next hole. If you are able to hit an opponent's marble lying in wait for its turn, you are able to place your marble up tight against the opponent's marble, flicking it hard and, hopefully, sending it way off course. This does, of course, put your opponent in a disadvantaged position. However, if your "flick" misses, there's a risk you could send your own marble flying off into no-man's land. The one sinking his marble into all four corner holes wins the game by being the first to get into the final hole in the middle. Victory! And the reward: you get to keep all the marbles being used in the game by your friends. Sweet, sweet victory!

So where did we put our spoils from knuckling down? Yep—you guessed it—they went right into our old, worn marble bag. After the game, we would stand around, comparing our bags of marbles. How big was yours compared to your friends', sometimes smaller, sometimes bigger? Comparing prized marbles—the steelie, the cat's eye, the crystal, the albino. What a game!

Marbles was a high-risk game at that age and we were careful with which marbles we played. A lot of our marbles were very special (an unusual crystal, a small steelie, a bright solid colour). We carried them around in that marble bag, took them out to admire them, or showed them to our friends before, inevitably, we took a chance and knuckled down with that rare steelie or albino, with the risk that it could become part of someone else's prized collection.

And then ... we grew up. But funny how life has turned out to be an advanced version of marbles. At the risk of being too cynical, as a society, we run our whole lives trying to win at what is, at its core, a game of marbles: that promotion, starting a new business, being one of the top salespeople, measuring up, keeping up. Funny how the development of our competitive instincts as kids becomes such a powerful influence in our adult lives.

We subtly (or, sadly, not so subtly) compare marbles. How big is your bag of marbles (networth)? Check out my steelie (my expensive car). How about this rare cat's eye (my impressive house)? Have you seen my beautiful albino (my holiday property)? And many carry their "bag of marbles" around like medals on a war hero's chest.

We call these Treasure Marbles. We collect these marbles, sometimes earning them through our employment, sometimes by starting a business. And sometimes we do not even have to earn them. We inherit them, find ourselves in the right place at the right time with a lucky business deal, or even win a lottery.

We can collect, spend, trade, or give away Treasure Marbles as we choose. This game of collecting and spending Treasure Marbles often consumes the majority of our adult lives. Thankfully, for most of us, the novelty of the Treasure Marble game will eventually wear off. We feel satisfied with our networth and start to wonder about our *Lifeworth*.

Lifeworth is the time when some people have a sense of what is "enough" for material comforts, and are now deriving satisfaction more from personal involvements and experiences. The people who have found more value in *Lifeworth* rather than networth are known for taking on challenges or risks and are giving back to the world in a significant, sustainable, and meaningful way. Not everyone will find the true wealth in *Lifeworth*—many, but not everyone.

We want to be perfectly clear on one point: it is not inherently wrong to collect Treasure Marbles. Networth is a necessary and, for the most part, enjoyable part of our lives. We all need these marbles to sustain our lives and to meet our needs and wants. The amount we choose to collect varies greatly from person to person in all walks of life. What we are suggesting is that there is something beyond networth, and that networth can open up opportunities for *Lifeworth* experiences.

There are at least two other types of marbles in our bag besides Treasure Marbles. We can also find Talent Marbles and Time Marbles in our bags. Talent Marbles are ones we both collect and distribute at will. Talent might be something we are born with, perhaps a talent in the arts, music, sports, woodworking, or metalworking. It may be something that, although learned, comes easily to a person. The more we practice this talent, the better our skills become and the more Talent Marbles we are able to put in our bags.

Talent might also come through a career: being good with numbers, adept with surgical instruments, or talented at organizing and managing people. Talent can come in many different forms, and what one person is good at, another may not be. An engineer can design an upgrader for the oil sands.

An instrumentation technician can have an entire building or plant running through advanced software programs. Another person would not have a clue. One person might be brilliant with construction, while another can help people with addictions find their way back to a better life. Talent comes in many different packages. It's a gift that can be channelled into helping other people. Instead of just using their talents to gather more Treasure Marbles, some people channel their Talent Marbles for the betterment of other people's lives. They say, "Hey, I can help them find good water and develop that water system for their village," or, "I can help build that school for kids in a country that desperately needs them." "I can raise money and organize people for the shelter in my home town to help the less-fortunate." Giving away Talent Marbles runs to the core of our humanity.

Unlike Treasure and Talent Marbles, Time Marbles are not collected, just spent. When we are born into this world, we are given a defined, but un-known, number of Time Marbles. These marbles are placed in our bags at birth and every minute, every hour, every day, we must give up some of our Time Marbles. It is automatic and it can't be stopped. Our Time Marbles are never replenished, just spent. You can't collect, hoard, or trade Time Marbles. The only control we have on our Time Marbles is *how* they are used.

We would like you to remember this special number: 1,440. This is the number of minutes in each day of our lives. These are non-bankable minutes! How we use them is an important facet of our lives, but we can't save any minutes from this day to carry over to a future day. They just keep ticking away. We can't stop their steady flow out of our bags. There is a predeter-mined amount, a predetermined rate of depletion with a finite time period. Everyone's depletion rate is the same. We can decide how we want to spend or use our Time Marbles as we please. We just don't know how long it will take for the last Time Marble to drop out of our personal marble bag. We decide where these marbles will go and whom they will benefit. Spending our Time Marbles as we please with focused intention takes us to the root of life. It's the basis of being on-purpose, goal-oriented, content, and fulfilled. This is where *Lifeworth* begins. People with fewer Treasure Marbles and perhaps fewer Talent Marbles can live as enriching a life as people who have more Treasure and Talent Marbles. Time is the common thread.

For mental clarity, we decided to add some colour to these marbles. Time Marbles are red, because, sooner or later in our lives, time takes on a sense of urgency. Treasure Marbles are green. It is not too difficult to connect the colour green to money. We chose blue for the Talent Marbles to represent growth and vitality (and it was the only remaining primary colour!).

We learn the value of marbles and the marble-collecting game at an early age. In the first half of our lives, we compete for Talent and Treasure Marbles. Usually, the Talent Marbles experience a net flow into our marble bag. We develop skills, recognize talents, and gain experience and education, each with specific uses or purposes. At this point, we are trying to survive the game of marbles by improving our Talent Marbles and collecting Treasure Marbles.

As we continue to compete for marbles and our collection becomes more valuable—more marbles, better marbles, hard-to-collect marbles—we begin to measure our self-worth by what we have accomplished. As our Talent and Treasure Marbles increase, part of our self-esteem and self-worth grows. This is the part of our self-esteem that requires recognition and approval from outside of ourselves, from those around us. This is sometimes referred to as external self-esteem. In varying degrees, it is an important part of who we are.

As we gaze upon our collection and see how many of each type of marble we have, there is another simple principle that affects our perception of our prized marble collection—the scarcity-abundance principle. It has an impact on almost every aspect of our lives.

The "scarcity" part of the principle assumes that there is only so much of a particular item or resource available. Whenever someone else gets some of that item, it is assumed that there is potentially less for us, or anyone else, to share. As other people collect their marbles, we fear that there will be fewer marbles for us to collect. As people collect or view their marbles with the scarcity mentality, they can become much less willing to part with them or to share them.

The "abundance" part of the principle is exactly the opposite. Abundance assumes that there is always enough of something to go around. As other people collect their marbles, we are confident that there will still be more than enough marbles for ourselves and for others to collect. When someone else achieves a sales goal or experiences a new success, this does not diminish our opportunity to achieve our sales goal or successes. There is enough for everyone.

Scarcity and abundance are two ends of the same stick, with thousands of points in between. And here is the odd thing about this stick: each of us can choose where we are on the stick and how we view our world from this point. Does this have an impact on our bag of marbles? Big time! We can collect—and spend, lose, or give away—marbles from a scarcity mentality. We have to hurry up and collect and keep all we can for ourselves and for our family. This part of life is much more of a competition for resources, a competition for Talent and Treasure Marbles, and we may be less willing to give up very much. Think of the old T-shirt slogan: "He who dies with the most toys wins." This perspective is generally reinforced as we go through the middle parts of our lives and careers.

The abundance view of our bag of marbles is quite different. We recognize when we have sufficient marbles to meet our current and future needs, and the needs of those important to us. Yes, collecting marbles is still important to us, but we are more willing to share what is in our bag, because we know we can always acquire more. This view is more of a collaborative point of view. We recognize that we can create larger impacts by being willing to share our marbles with others. The fact that others are also collecting their marbles does not diminish our ability to collect the ones we need. Maybe the revised T-shirt motto could read: "He who shares the most toys wins."

We have a choice of how we view our bag of marbles—through the scarcity lens, the abundance lens, or someplace in between. This has a direct effect on how we live our lives and how we relate to others. Neither end of the stick is inherently better than the other. As in any part of life, going to either extreme can result in unintended consequences. It is important for each of us to find our balance point on the stick for that point in our lives. We also need to understand that this balance point can shift, depending on our circumstances at any point in time.

There is a constantly shifting balance of each type of marble in our marble bags. The ratio of red ones to blue ones to green ones is continually changing. There is an imbalance of marbles in our bag as we begin life. All of our red Time Marbles are put into the bag from the start—this represents the time we have to live our lives until we die. When we first look into the bag, we see almost all red Time Marbles, a few blue Talent Marbles, and almost no green Treasure Marbles (other than maybe a few monetary gifts from grandparents, aunts, or uncles). This is what we start out with, and the net flow for Time Marbles is out of the bag. Each and every day, there is a stream of red marbles leaving our marble bag. We can't add more Time Marbles to the bag. In the beginning, our Treasure and Talent Marbles are very limited compared to our Time Marbles. In our pre-adult years, it seems quite easy to reach into our bag to find our Time Marbles; time seems to be an unlimited quantity. It is more difficult to find the Treasure or Talent Marbles in these early years. Every day, we spend Time Marbles effortlessly. Their abundance makes them easy to spend or lose in the marble game.

As we pursue our careers, raise our families, and explore our world through the middle years of our lives, we add more green and blue marbles to our bag. The ratio of red to green to blue begins to change. We may see similar numbers of red, blue, and green marbles. It might be difficult to easily identify what we have more of. The marbles seem to arrive at a balance—barely enough Time Marbles, enough Talent Marbles for now, and enough Treasure Marbles to stay in our comfort zone. It is also a time when it might become a bit more difficult to quickly find our red Time Marbles. Ironically, these are also the years when we physically begin to feel the time crunch: getting kids to activities, meetings, work, personal activities, volunteer activities, etc.

At some point in each of our lives, this balance changes. We have enough Treasure Marbles to meet our current and future needs, and so we begin to examine how we use the rest of our marbles. We begin to recognize that Time Marbles are no longer the most-abundant marbles. The value of the marbles begins to shift ever so slightly, sometimes without our recognizing it. The Time Marbles become more valuable and we become less willing to use them wantonly. When we look into our bag, we see more and more green and blue marbles in comparison to the red marbles. At some point, we have these subconscious thoughts: "So what? What am I really here for? Why am I doing this? What is the purpose of all of the green marbles? What can I do with my blue and green marbles, before I run out of red marbles?"

Unfortunately, many of us unknowingly relinquish control and distribution of our Time Marbles. We get caught up in the busyness of life, which is not necessarily a bad thing. As society expects, we may marry, have children, start a career, or start a business. In short, we're just getting a life, and, during this part of our lives, we do lose some degree of control over the spending of our Time Marbles.

Of course, we are happy with the time we have spent or are spending raising a family and developing a career or business. These are some of the good times, some of our best times, when great memories are created, lasting relationships are formed, and nest eggs are built. And, as life would have it, there will come a time when this part of our lives will fade and become part of our past. We will look into life's rear-view mirror and smile at what has happened, remembering the good times and the not-so-good, growing from life's highs and lows.

Then our gaze will once again move away from the rear-view mirror. We will look forward in life to the next part of the journey, with renewed hope and vision. We'll wonder what the road ahead will hold for us. We'll continue to wonder, "How long until we get there?"—wherever *there* is. "How much further?"

Hopefully, the horizon holds excitement and wonder. And it is at this point that we start to wonder about the best way to spend the Time Marbles that are still slowly and continually leaving our marble bag. Every time we breathe in, every time we breathe out, a marble leaves our bag. "Were they well spent?" we will ask ourselves. "Did it make a difference in my life? Did it make a difference in the life of someone else?"

Oh, look, another marble just left our bag.

Then, we all come to the end of the game of life and are launched into overtime. And, right after we die, imagine our bags of marbles being lifted up and summarily dumped onto a well-polished concrete floor. Ever seen that with a real bag of marbles? It's wild! The marbles bounce and scatter all over the place and a sense of panic sets in: "I'm losing my marbles. Somebody else is going to get my marbles."

The same is true of our "life" marbles. Family, friends, government, creditors, and charities will all be going wild trying to get as many of our marbles as they can. Of course, it is only our Treasure Marbles they will be fighting over. Our Talent Marbles run out when we "run out," and one of our goals should be to use up all of our talents before this happens. And, obviously, the last of our Time Marbles has left our bag.

The feeding frenzy for our Treasure Marbles only lasts for a very short while, and all the marbles we have collected throughout our life are redistributed. In a snap of a finger and the last bounce of a marble, they're all gone—they're now in someone else's bag. And the cycle continues, decade after decade, generation after generation. The game is as endless as time itself. And it is just that, a game.

So what's the message in all this? It's not that the real-life game of marbles we play is bad—not at all! But the fact is that it *is* just a game. What we do with our marbles is important. What difference can our marbles make in the lives of others, now and in overtime after we are gone? How we plan for the redistribution of our marbles is critical. It helps define our *Lifeworth,* rather than our networth.

No one can predict the future, but one thing is certain: we will all lose all of our marbles at the end of the game, and we will all leave a legacy of some type, whether intentional or not. A legacy is created not only while we're here but also after we're gone. Losing our marbles helps frame the fact that our life was well-lived, that someone will know decades after we are gone that we even spent time on Earth. The legacy we leave can have an impact several generations into the future. And the great thing is that we can choose to influence the type of legacy we leave. ■

SO NOW WHAT?

So far we have equated life with a bag of marbles that we collect, spend, lose, share, and prize over our lifetime. We have introduced you quite literally to three types of marbles in our lives: Time Marbles, Talent Marbles, and Treasure Marbles. You should now have a mental image of this colourful, well-worn bag of red, green, and blue marbles that is changing constantly over your lifetime.

So what does this really have to do with life? We feel that the bag of marbles is our currency for playing in the game of life. Marbles are important tools in meeting our needs, achieving our wants, and growing personally.

- What marbles are you currently collecting?

- How will you use your marbles?

- What can you do with the marbles in your marble bag to create your own life worth living as you may define it or to help others achieve theirs?

- If you looked into your marble bag right now, what colour would you see the most of?

- Which one of the three types of marbles is truly the most important to you? Why?

CHAPTER TWO

JESSE'S JOURNEY

—JOHN DAVIDSON

A rock pile ceases to be a rock pile the moment a single man contemplates it, bearing within him the image of a cathedral.

ANTOINE DE SAINT-EXUPERY

A splendid thing happened to John and Sherene Davidson on April 10, 1980. Their son Jesse came into their lives. Little did they realize the impact their child would have on them and on others. Raised in London, Ontario, with his older brother, Tyler, and younger brother, Tim, Jesse was diagnosed in 1986 with Duchenne muscular dystrophy, a life-threatening condition that affects boys almost exclusively. Jesse was six years old. Few survive beyond their teens.

In 1995, at age fifteen, Jesse became recognized across Canada for his courage and determination through the charity that quickly became known as Jesse's Journey. Jesse's father, John, who was forty-nine years old at the time, pushed Jesse in his wheelchair 3,300 kilometres across Ontario, as part of a fundraiser that generated $1.5 million to fund research into a cure for Duchenne muscular dystrophy. When father and son returned home from that ordeal, the Toronto Maple Leafs asked Jesse to drop the ceremonial puck during the season's opening night at Maple Leaf Gardens in Toronto.

Jesse had previously met with Prime Minister Jean Chrétien and received a standing ovation in the House of Commons. In 1996, Jesse received the Order of Ontario and, a year later, he met Queen Elizabeth II at a tree-planting ceremony in London, Ontario. In 1998, Jesse flew to Paris, France, to assist the French Muscular Dystrophy Association (Association Francaise contra les Myopathies) with its thirty-hour telethon, not an easy task for someone in a wheelchair. The telethon generated $116 million CDN.

Jesse's Journey has provided the research community with more than $3 million in funding and the Jesse Davidson Endowment, which continues to fund research, has now surpassed $7 million. John wrote and released his first book, *Jesse's Journey: A Canadian Story*, in 2001. His second book, *The Right Road: How Far Will You Go?*, was published in 2010. Mike Sheffar, of Sheffar, Potter and Muchan, referred John to us. Here is John Davidson in his own words.

● ● ● ●

I n the first half of my life, I worked in the media, starting in radio after high school in Woodstock, Ontario. My early days in radio reminded me of the jokes you hear from media people who like to talk about how "it all started at a little 10,000-watt station in the Midwest." I guess my Midwest was Woodstock, Ontario.

I came to London [Ontario] in 1967. It was Centennial year and after my wife, Sherene, and I were married, we moved to Vancouver, where I was working in both radio and television at CBC. That was where I had the good fortune of working with people like Foster Hewitt and Danny Gallivan when the Leafs and Canadiens came west to play the Canucks. It was a great experience. I was able to take part in the historic 1972 Canada-Russia hockey series, meeting and interviewing people like Paul Henderson, who scored that famous series-winning goal in Moscow. When we decided to have a family, we came back to London, where we were more comfortable. I guess home is where the heart is. After working in radio and television for thirty years, I "escaped" from the media world. I've been with Jesse's Journey ever since.

And now, I'd like to tell you a story. It's a story about how a little boy changed the lives of so many people. It began in 1986 when our second son, Jesse, was diagnosed with Duchenne muscular dystrophy, a life-threatening disease for which there is no cure. When you receive that kind of news, your world flips upside-down. Suddenly, you're aware that you are in a race with time. For the next twenty-five years, we fought as hard as we could. On the morning of November 6, 2009, we lost Jesse when he was just twenty-nine years old, and we found that time had suddenly changed again. For our family, there was no longer a need to hurry. It was that second change in time that allowed me to shift gears a little bit as I looked back at what Jesse had accomplished.

In the years that followed Jesse's diagnosis, we reached a point where both Sherene and I were needed around the house. When it took two of us to do the lifting and moving, I just couldn't say, "I'll see you, Honey. I'm going to play golf for five or six hours. I'll be back later." Instead, I put the golf clubs in the garage and I didn't touch them for ten years. But I wanted to stay in shape, so I took up walking. I would walk in our neighbourhood and I got to see how people stacked the wood in their garages, who hung their bicycles up neatly in the winter and who didn't. I even got to know most of the neighbourhood dogs by name!

The years went by and the walks kept getting longer, to the point where Sherene would drop me off in the country and I'd just walk home. As the walks grew in time and distance, it dawned on me one day that maybe we could turn this walking into something. It was quite surreal, because here I was taking up walking at a time when Jesse was losing his ability to walk.

I was still trying to come to terms with the realization that life was going to be different. We were the parents of a youngster who wasn't going to play on a hockey team or a baseball team. He wasn't going to drive a car, and, in my quietest moments, it broke my heart to realize there probably wasn't going to be that dreamed-of wedding day in June. But somewhere inside me I still felt that Jesse was destined to do something very special in life.

The clock kept ticking louder and louder with each passing day while the walking continued. The idea of turning this walking into something never left my mind, and more and more I found myself along the side of the road, walking, thinking, and wondering. A dream was starting to take shape that would see Jesse and me go across Ontario, with me pushing my son in his wheelchair. We would shake as many hands as possible and tell people about a terrible disease that robs parents of their children. I wondered if we could maybe raise $100,000 to support research.

On his fourteenth birthday, I shared my idea with Jesse and asked him to think about it before giving me an answer. Just like his mother, Jesse usually took things "under advisement" before reaching a decision. Jesse knew that I was serious and that I wasn't nuts. Well, maybe not *completely* nuts. Just over a year later, I began pushing my son in his wheelchair as we set out on what would be the adventure of a lifetime.

It was a cold Saturday morning in May 1995 when we started our journey together at the Ontario-Manitoba border, 54 kilometres west of Kenora, Ontario. That was the beginning, and the rest is history. We didn't raise $100,000. We raised $1.5 million for research. There were times when I was tired, but the die had been cast long before we took to the road and I knew that quitting was not an option. When Jesse was up and ready to go day after day, I thought to myself, "If Jesse is ready to go, then what excuse do I have?" And so, day after day, we pushed on down the road toward the Ontario-Quebec border—3,300 kilometres away.

I was tethered to Jesse's wheelchair by a safety harness that clipped to my belt, just in case I fell. Like a lot of what we were doing, we were making it up as we went. The tether idea would let me become Jesse's anchor and prevent him from rolling away from me, especially on the monster hills of Northern Ontario. We may have been making some things up as we went, but the important thing is that we made a start. Whatever your dream may be, you have to start somewhere. While our four-month journey across Ontario was a tremendous challenge, it was a great adventure for a youngster who represented so many youngsters who never get to have an adventure.

After 124 days on the road, we completed our journey at the Ontario-Quebec border in Ottawa and we came home to London in late September, four months after we began. Driving home, I was alone with the thought that I could do more. I kept that secret to myself, knowing that I would try again. I knew that, the next time, I would take on a bigger challenge in doing everything I could to fight a disease that robs parents of their children.

The clock was still ticking as I contemplated what I thought of as Jesse's Journey, Part II. I knew that if I was going to take on an even bigger challenge, the decision had to be made soon. I was over fifty when I committed to walking across Canada and the plans moved onto the drawing board. This time, the journey would be without Jesse, but it would definitely be *for* Jesse. This was a journey that would take ten months, crossing six and a half time zones, and it would include parts of two winters. It would be too much to ask of Jesse.

After seven months of training, I dipped my running shoes in the Atlantic Ocean at Quidi Vidi, Newfoundland, on Jesse's birthday, April 10, 1998, and took to the road again. Ten months later, I dipped those same shoes in the Pacific Ocean, in Beacon Hill Park in Victoria, British Columbia. There were awards and honours that followed, like being recognized by the *Guinness Book of World Records* for a record-setting 286-day walk across Canada. But what really mattered was our raising another $2 million for research and launching the Jesse Davidson Endowment, which has since grown to more than $7 million. I'm still amazed by what can happen when a human being sets his or her mind to something. The boundaries are endless. The effects of that walk across our nation sparked other families afflicted with Duchenne to get involved with Jesse's Journey. Nudged out of their own comfort zones, where they may have been stalled with a sense of loss and not knowing where to turn, they came to realize what could be accomplished when people try hard. For more than ten years since the walk across Canada, I have shared our story with thousands of people in audiences in Canada and abroad. I still have a deep desire to share our story and to encourage and inspire people to *reach for their dream*.

Losing Jesse was the most difficult thing I have ever faced. Speaking to people about what is possible in life, about what Jesse managed to accomplish, and the legacy he left, helps me keep my son alive in my heart.

When families just like ours are at the beginning of their journey with their little boy who has Duchenne muscular dystrophy, it's important to them, when they reach out for comfort and support to Jesse's Journey, to know that it is probably Canada's smallest and hardest-working charity. Those moms and dads know that I'm someone who's been down the road they now find themselves on. I'm always willing to listen and to provide hope in whatever way I can. I want them to know that, more than anything, I intend to carry on in order to help their son. I think it's what Jesse would want me to do. When a new family contacts Jesse's Journey, I often ask them if it would be helpful if I came to see them. While they are usually surprised that I'm willing to do that, I've found it makes a world of difference to people to know that they are not alone.

When people come to know us and realize how hard we work to see that research is funded, that work ethic rubs off, and then they want to do something. Oftentimes, they want to become a part of "Walk Across Canada in a Day," our major annual fundraising event. Sometimes, they want to organize things like a car rally or a golf tournament. They want to do everything in their power to improve the quality of their children's lives. They begin to feel that infectious sense of accomplishment, a sense that they are on the front lines in the fight to rid the world of an insidious disease that wreaks havoc on families. Their desire to help becomes contagious, and they appreciate the transparency at Jesse's Journey, where they can see their efforts funding research. Jesse's Journey was recently acknowledged in the *New England Journal of Medicine* for its funding of research projects in Canada and the United States. The day that I saw the little charity that Jesse and I had started being acknowledged in print … I wished Jesse could have been here to see how our dream has grown.

Life often delivers us peak experiences, intended or otherwise. Sometimes it's a positive experience, and sometimes it's a negative experience. In my lifetime, I have twice experienced a positive peak experience. Both our journeys were planned, intentional, and most definitely positive. That was the way it was from the first day to our last day in crossing Ontario together, and then on my solo journey across Canada. When it comes to being fulfilled, I can't pick one journey over the other, because there were thousands of individual experiences during both of the times that I was on the road. I kept a journal that I wrote in every night, because I thought, if I don't capture this experience, it will just fade away with time. I captured everything I could, and I came to realize that if your life is worth living, it's worth writing down.

Both trips were full of hundreds and hundreds of peak positive experiences, and they didn't have to be huge things to make an impact on my life. They were gold nuggets, and each and every one was meaningful. They were things like someone putting a little guardian angel pin in your hand. This happened all the time. These were people who probably lost a relative, or perhaps a child. I seldom learned the details of their story. I can still remember how they would squeeze one of these tiny pins into my hand with such emotion and love. It was things like that or something a little kid would say to you in such a matter-of-fact way in asking about Jesse. Kids are amazing, because they have no agenda; they just want to help. At times, it was overwhelming.

When I look back on our road adventures, I think my greatest joy was in seeing the positive manner in which Jesse reacted to those peak experiences. Jesse represented a group that so often doesn't get to have any peak experiences. I think he was pretty thrilled when we were at centre ice at Maple Leaf Gardens on opening night after our journey across Ontario. The drums and bagpipes of the 48th Highlanders were echoing in our chests as the teams lined up on their respective blue lines and fireworks lit up the darkness while spotlights danced across the on-ice festivities. There were pencil-thin laser lights cutting through the darkness, and the house lights slowly came up as Jesse and I, dressed in tuxedos, took part in the ceremonial puck drop to start the season.

Doug Gilmore, the Toronto Maple Leafs' captain at that time, pushed Jesse to centre ice in his wheelchair. I had cautioned Doug to be careful, because the wheelchair could tip very easily. The chair, which came from St. Louis, was custom-made of titanium and was extremely light. I'll never forget when Doug leaned in for that ceremonial faceoff and said to Jesse and me, "You guys are doing a really great thing." It was another of those peak experiences for the memory box.

Receiving the Order of Ontario from the province's Lieutenant-Governor was a great honour for Jesse and, as a dad, I don't think I could have been prouder on that night. You have to remember that we are talking about a youngster who couldn't walk or run, never used a skateboard, couldn't swim, and had never ridden a bicycle. For Jesse, who had never been on a hockey or baseball team, this was his "all-star" moment. There were other peak experience moments, like meeting Queen Elizabeth II and Canada's prime minister at the time, the Honourable Jean Chretien. Jesse just shone on those occasions. It was so heart-warming to be there and to see and share in those special peak experiences in his life.

Sometimes people ask me what comes next? I will keep building the foundation that Jesse and I started. We began with a dream that one day we would be able to leave a million dollars a year for as long as it takes to find a cure. A million dollars will buy a lot of research, especially when that money is leveraged. Canadians are not quite as good as our American neighbours at leveraging research dollars, but we're getting better at it. Globally, the research community seems to have found Jesse's Journey, and we receive more grant applications than ever before. In each of the last two years, we have been able to provide the research community with $500,000 from the Jesse Davidson Endowment, and I would like to see our ability to do that continue to grow.

I guess if the good Lord lets me stick around a little longer, then maybe I'll get to see us reach the point where we can leave a million a year, every year, forever. That's our goal—to provide money for research into a cure for Duchenne muscular dystrophy—and to help us reach that goal I have taken up a new career. I have written a book called *The Right Road,* and I use our story to talk about our dream and your potential dreams. I really want to share our story with people and encourage them to pursue that dream that's inside them. I have met thousands of people who want to do things like run for office, learn to play the cello, speak Spanish, or become a volunteer. I want to help them reach that goal. My plan is to speak to as many corporate audiences as possible so that we can make life better for a pretty special group of young people who have very limited ability to do things on their own. Providing Canadians from coast to coast with positive peak experiences is what I want to do each and every day.

I have been very fortunate in my life. I can honestly say that I have only had one problem in my lifetime, and I have been lucky enough to have a chance to work on that problem every day. I would like to be remembered as an inspiration to people and someone who tried his best and who let people know that you can do anything you want if you put your mind to it. Jesse never let being in a wheelchair stop him from doing the things he wanted to do in life. People with disabilities of all kinds saw

Jesse as a champion. He taught people that you can get a job. You can go to school. You can learn, and you can help others have those positive peak experiences that enrich lives.

When he went to school, Jesse grew up with kids from all over the world, and they showed how much they cared for each other by the way they cared for him. When Jesse was about nine years old and nearing the end of his ability to walk, he began to fall a lot. That no-nonsense attitude that kids have was very visible when his friends would just pick Jesse up and, together, they would carry on. Where do we lose that ability to reach out in life to help others? Why do we lose that ability? How can we keep those positive peak experiences happening throughout our lives?

I think people really want to stretch and reach for new things, new adventures, but they may be a little afraid. Fear is short for False Evidence Appearing Real. That unrealistic fear may have you thinking that you can't do things. The truth is, you can do all kinds of things. You can start by dreaming. The beautiful thing about dreaming is that the sky's the limit and you can dream as big as you want, financially or otherwise.

Jesse was a great role model who taught me that the greatest piece of mind is found in giving. When our little charity writes those cheques that are going to keep a researcher at the bench, it's very satisfying. There is a huge misperception that researchers make a lot of money. Most of them don't. They stay with what they are doing because they believe they are going to find something and that they are going to make a difference. That's their real motivation. That's what gives them a positive peak experience. It's not about the money. Hal and Dana have asked me what my definition of a life worth living might look like. I think that a life worth living is when you can fall asleep comfortably and quickly knowing that what you truly believe you're here to do is being done, and being done well.

We are just small flecks in the universe. We aren't here very long. Our time goes by pretty quickly. Go and do those things that you really, really want to do. If you're listening, that's the little voice that you hear when you put your head on the pillow at night. You always know in your heart when you're selling yourself short. Maybe you are one of those people who have yet to reach that level of fulfillment that you really want to reach. When you decide to reach for that dream of yours, you will be surprised how the positive peak experiences start going off like rockets all around you. You can start by slowing down, stepping back from what you're doing and taking a look at your life. Do a personal inventory of your strengths and weaknesses to help you chart your course. More than anything else, listen to where your heart wants you to go. Those positive peak experiences are waiting for you!

You may not be able to articulate it, but almost everyone knows they have a true purpose in life. Keep searching for yours. Learn from others. Continue reading books like this. Someday soon, your purpose for being here will be revealed to you. My son Jesse was the catalyst in my life who helped me find mine. ■

To learn more, visit www.jessesjourney.com

SO NOW WHAT?

During his story, John mentioned several peak experiences along the way, some small, some big, but all equally rewarding. He also mentioned conducting a personal inventory of your strengths and weaknesses, to take a look at your life, and to listen to your heart's direction.

- What emotions did you feel as you read John's compelling and personal story?

- What ideas or thoughts crept into your mind that could become the seeds of some peak experience in your future? What yearnings do you have that you might have felt even early in your childhood?

- What are your real strengths? What knowledge do you have that you excel at? What skills have you developed that you truly enjoy and are good at?

- What are your innate talents or natural abilities or aptitudes? What things come naturally or easily to you? How do you spontaneously respond to different situations?

- If there were no restrictions of any kind, what one or two things would you like to do that feel close to your unique purpose?

CHAPTER THREE

TRAPPED IN THE COMFORT ZONE

We cannot become what we want to be
by remaining what we are.

MAX DE PREE

Have you ever used the term "comfort zone" to describe a certain time in your life: a time when things seemed to be going smoothly, not too many peaks or valleys, not too much stress or anxiety? A time when you felt confident, safe, or comfortable in a particular situation? A time when you felt you were performing at your best? Did you ever decide not to do something because you felt it was outside of your comfort zone? Most of us experience these comfort zones at different times in our lives. But just what is the "Comfort Zone" and how does it differ from one person to another?

In Chapter 1, we introduced you to the concept of the bag of life marbles, a bag containing Treasure Marbles (green), Time Marbles (red), and Talent Marbles (blue). We told you how this bag of marbles is our currency for playing in the game of life. These marbles are important tools for meeting our basic needs, achieving our wants, and growing personally. In this chapter, we are going to look at the Comfort Zone from the perspective of our individual needs.

At our deepest psychological level, we are driven primarily by our needs and, to some extent, by our wants. We all have needs and wants of different types and degrees. Most human needs fall into three broad categories without diminishing their uniqueness. Our needs are one of our most basic motivators, the reasons we do certain things or behave in certain ways. Our behaviours and actions are designed to satisfy our needs and, to some degree, our wants. If we can begin to understand how these needs motivate us and the challenges we might face trying to satisfy them, we can begin to better understand our journey through life. We hope to help you see and understand one small part of this journey from a new and enriching perspective.

Our discussion of human needs is based loosely on the work of psychologist Clayton Alderfer. His ERG Theory of Needs, outlined in his book, *Existence, Relatedness, and Growth: Human Needs in Organizational Settings,* is very direct, simple, and flexible. It involves three levels of needs: Existence needs, Relationship needs, and Growth needs (ERG). We have adapted his terms and concepts to fit into a model of concentric circles that we will use to help us define the Comfort Zone. This model provides a simple overview of the various needs that motivate us throughout our lives. The circles in the model constantly emanate outward from ourselves at the centre.

Each circle represents a general category of common human needs. These needs are with us throughout our lives, constantly shifting, changing, and intersecting. At first glance, the circles in these figures appear distinct and unique. This is merely a way of modelling the three different types of needs. In reality, there are no true defining lines between them. The three circles are actually only somewhat distinct, only somewhat unique, and more dynamic than static. Together, they form our Comfort Zone, the zone where we are comfortably meeting and supporting the various needs (and wants) in those circles.

In our adaptation of Alderfer's theory, the innermost circle of the Comfort Zone represents our Existence needs. These refer to our concern with basic existence motivators, which can include, for example, food, water, air, shelter, clothing, safety, security, love, and affection. Existence needs are the easiest ones for us to recognize and satisfy because their objectives can be reduced to material or concrete "stuff" (you know, the stuff we all have in some form or another), very tangible and hands-on. For example, when we buy our first house, we can experience it in a very tangible way with all of our senses. We can smell the fresh paint, feel the grain of the wood on the cupboard doors, and see the freshly cut lawn in the backyard. When we purchase our weekly supply of groceries, we physically carry the bags home, we place the items in various cupboards, later

Figure 3.1

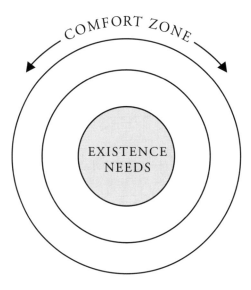

on we cook with them, and we eventually consume the meals we make, again experiencing this with all of our senses. When we buy a new toy or gadget, a new item of clothing, a book, or dinner out, we can also experience these things in a very tangible way with our senses. Our Existence needs are the most basic and concrete needs in our lives. It can be tough to live comfortably without meeting them.

The next circle moving outward represents our need for creating and maintaining interpersonal relationships, our Relationship needs. These are the needs involving relationships with significant others: our family, relatives, friends, colleagues, and our community. They represent the need to be recognized and appreciated, and to feel secure as part of a group, a family, or a culture. Satisfying these needs generates feelings of acceptance, belonging, and community, reinforced by interpersonal dynamics and interactions. It involves recognition by others of our efforts and achievements. We feel valued and appreciated. This is the area in which we find achievement, status, responsibility, reputation, affection,

Figure 3.2

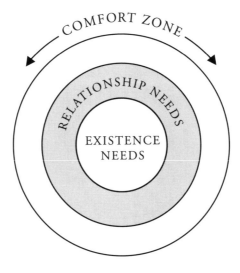

and fulfilling relationships. Part of our self-esteem, sometimes referred to as external self-esteem, is achieved in this area. It is dependent, in part, upon communication from, and interaction with, others.

Relationship needs are less concrete and tangible than are Existence needs. There can be more uncertainty involved, and it can be more difficult to recognize when we satisfy these needs. For example, your employer may provide you with little or no feedback on the quality of your work. You wonder if he or she is satisfied with your performance. This can create more uncertainty than a boss who provides you with direct feedback on your performance. The satisfaction of this particular need in this example depends on the type of relationship and communication you have with your employer.

The third circle represents our Growth needs, our intrinsic desire for personal development, to gain the skills, knowledge, talents, and experiences we need to be successful in life. Our individual growth generally comes from embracing learning and experiences that call on us to fully utilize and develop our capacities. We become educated in different ways,

Figure 3.3

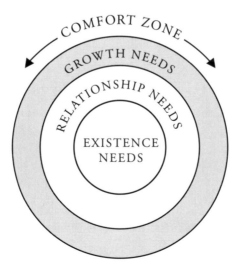

develop new skills and talents, and explore new experiences that contribute to our growth and development as a person. Most often this growth relates to our career development, our development as parents, our development in personal pursuits, and our development in relationships with others (e.g., family, community, work).

Growth needs have specific objectives that depend on the uniqueness of each person. Satisfaction of Growth needs occurs when we do and experience things that enhance, enrich, or enlarge our ability to function successfully in meeting all of our needs. This can occur as a result of success or failure in attaining predetermined goals. Recognizing when and how well we satisfy these needs is, once again, more difficult than the previous level, the Relationship needs. Growth needs are much less concrete and much more intangible. There can be a greater degree of uncertainty involved in trying to, first, identify them and, second, satisfy them in a meaningful way. For example, you may have an innate ability to draw and people have commented on your doodles and sketches. You may have a deep desire to explore and develop more of your artistic skills. What will this look like? Will you learn how to paint landscapes? Will you take a class in live-model sketching? Will you learn how to create computer graphics to illustrate your ideas? Once you start down one of these avenues, will it fully satisfy your Growth need in the artistic area, or will it become a lifelong pursuit of excellence?

There is no particular order to these three levels of needs. There is usually a continued need to maintain our basic Existence needs at our desired level. Beyond that, we generally have multiple needs to satisfy at the same time. Needs in different circles may motivate an individual simultaneously and different types of needs can be pursued alongside each other. For example, you may be taking a rock climbing course to explore your passion for outdoor adventure (Growth needs) while at the same time you continue to maintain the important relationships in your life (Relationship needs) and keep up with the mortgage and car payments, buy groceries and necessities, pay school and sports fees, medical bills, etc. (Existence needs). The order of needs that an individual focuses on can differ from one person to another. The needs we concentrate on change at different points in our lives.

The boundaries of each area are constantly shifting, requiring different levels of ongoing energy and focus, sometimes called "maintenance energy." This is the energy we need to maintain our current spot in the Comfort Zone we have established.

Remember the Time Marbles, Treasure Marbles, and Talent Marbles? Well, here is where they come into play (so to speak). Our needs are constant motivators throughout our lives and require at least a minimum number of marbles to maintain the Comfort Zone in which we choose to live. The greater our needs or wants in the Comfort Zone, the more marbles are required to achieve and maintain them. For example, the size, style, quality, and location of the house we choose to live in can range from a simple one-bedroom apartment to a modest bungalow to a huge mansion in an exclusive neighbourhood. Each of them requires a different amount of all three types of marbles: Treasure Marbles to pay the bills, Time Marbles to earn enough Treasure Marbles, and Talent Marbles so we can earn enough income to maintain our current level.

Whatever the size of our Comfort Zone, regardless of whether it is built around actual needs or perceived wants, once we have developed its boundaries, we need to be able to constantly maintain those boundaries, and it requires sufficient Time, Talent, and Treasure Marbles to be able to do that. To expand our Comfort Zone would require more marbles of some type in our bag. Having fewer marbles of any type will require us to reduce the size of our Comfort Zone, because we cannot support it.

The Comfort Zone represents the bulk of the game of life, as we know it. We are constantly collecting, acquiring, saving, spending, and giving away our three types of marbles in this zone. We are forever shifting the areas where we place different types of marbles on the Comfort Zone game board. We work out systems that meet some of our needs (e.g., Existence needs) in such a way that they do not require our full attention, thus freeing up energy for higher-level needs. For example, how much time do you spend thinking about your basic living costs (food, utilities, housing, etc.)? Probably not too much, because you have worked out automatic systems for dealing with these needs. This allows you time to focus on needs in any of the three categories (e.g., taking an annual holiday with your family, enrolling in a self-improvement course). We move in and out of the different areas of our Comfort Zone as circumstances and support structures in our lives change. For example, if there is a serious illness or death of someone close to us, Relationship needs tend to become very important at that time. We tend to focus less on our Existence and Growth needs and direct more of our energy to our loved ones, at least temporarily.

Our ability to move in and out of the different areas is also partly related to the number and types of marbles in our bag. Sometimes, we don't have the right Talent Marbles or enough Time or Treasure Marbles to achieve needs at the outer areas. We may have to spend time trading and collecting more marbles in order to meet those needs.

As we have all experienced, changes to the Comfort Zone can come about through positive or negative events in our lives that affect the amount and ratio of marbles we have. We can decide to spend some of our Treasure Marbles on a holiday, or save some for a new house. We can spend some Treasure Marbles developing and acquiring new Talent Marbles in order to hopefully gain more Treasure Marbles. We can choose to use some of our Time Marbles (and maybe Talent Marbles) helping others meet some of the core needs in their lives.

At any point in time, you only have so many of each type of marble in your bag and all three types of needs require marbles for both maintenance and exploration. In order to meet all of our different needs, we need to shift where we use the marbles. Maybe we'll spend less on groceries in order to save for a holiday or that special gift. Maybe we'll spend time improving our golf score rather than painting the house. If we don't want to

shift our marbles around, then we have to add Talent and Treasure Marbles
to meet our needs and wants.

It is easy to see how the need to maintain our Comfort Zone can sometimes trap us there. We spend a great deal of the three types of marbles just
meeting all of our current needs and wants. Sometimes there is enough left
over to help push at the boundaries of our Comfort Zone but not enough
to break out of it. The Comfort Zone becomes exactly that: comfortable,
safe, secure, little risk, happy, smooth, not too many peaks and valleys.

But there is more to life than maintaining the Comfort Zone. There
is another zone that exists just on the outside edge of the Comfort Zone.
It is a zone of creativity, risk, stretching, trepidation, fear, and achievement. There are ways to stretch our Comfort Zones into this new zone,
if we want to. Our Comfort Zone can become either our best platform
for, or our biggest barrier to, achieving a peak experience. Sometimes it
takes a peak experience beyond our control to help us shake up the
boundaries of our Comfort Zone. We will explore this in more detail in
Chapter 5. ■

SO NOW WHAT?

Our Comfort Zone is defined by how confident, safe, and secure we are in meeting and achieving our needs at a particular
point in time. It feels like a safe place to be, and it feels like a
place you are capable of maintaining for now. But here is a challenge:

• What are you not doing or not achieving because you are tucked comfortably in your Comfort Zone?

- Why are you not achieving these things? How important is it that you achieve them?

- Are all of the needs that consume your current marbles truly *needs*, or are some of them *wants?*

- Can you shift some of your marbles around to expand beyond your Comfort Zone?

CHAPTER FOUR

GIDDY UP FOR WISHES

—MARTHA BIRKETT

No hour of life is wasted
that is spent in the saddle.

WINSTON CHURCHILL

Martha Birkett is an accomplished horsewoman from Cochrane, Alberta, a ranching community northwest of Calgary. She has three daughters, one stepdaughter, and one stepson, as well as four grandchildren. Along with her daughters, she owns two yoga studios and centres for healing, one in Red Deer and one in Cochrane called The Amaryllis Centre Inc.

At age forty-seven, Martha wanted to do something to help children in need. Out of the blue, she woke up one morning and decided to ride a horse from Ottawa to Cochrane to bring awareness to, and raise money for, the Children's Wish Foundation. Her ride, Giddy Up for Wishes, took place in 2008. It took Martha nearly four months, six days a week, averaging six to eight hours in the saddle, every day. Why would someone want to do that? Here is Martha in her own words.

• • • •

I come from a farming family of nine kids, all born one year apart. We worked on the farm, which was very hard work. We would often take in foster children, sometimes five at a time. Most had health issues: physical, mental, and emotional challenges. We would take all these kids in to help them through their troubled times. I recall at a young age being very motherly to them. I remember lying in bed at night, saying prayers and asking God to help me make a difference in their lives.

When I look back now, I was just a kid myself, but didn't give it any more thought than that. One of my sisters was severely handicapped, physically and mentally, and ended up in a home for the disabled. We would go to the home as a family to visit her. There were all these kids with different challenges, and I used to just love going there to spend time and play with them. Growing up, I lived in a home with so many kids and, when I got married, we had kids immediately. My life was filled with children.

In 1992, we had a life-changing experience. It would help to alter my life's goals through its huge impact. When my girls were six, ten, and twelve, we had a house fire. At the time, we lived in the bush way out in the country, just northwest of Lodgepole, Alberta. It was quite the remote way of life, though a way that encourages a strong bond between a mother and her daughters.

On September 17 of that year, I happened to be putting in a twelve-hour day working for the Alberta Forest Service as this was my last seasonal work day; no more work until spring. I decided to bring my children to a babysitter who lived on the AFS compound until I was done my long day (a definite blessing, as they weren't home when the tragedy struck). I picked them up and we headed home at dusk. There was a glowing hue in the sky and, the closer I got to home, the brighter it was. When I turned the final corner, I came upon our house and out-buildings, all engulfed in a fiery inferno. The children hid their faces in the back seat.

I had to turn around and drive back into town, about thirty kilome-tres, to call the fire department. I raced back to the house, but by the time everyone arrived, it was too late. It had burned to the ground and we lost everything. We had nothing but the clothes we were wearing. That was it. We also lost some animals in the fire. The horses were able to escape, but a litter of kittens and two dogs perished. We spent some time nursing two cats to health after some burns, and sadly watched our family dog deteriorate after the traumatic event. We had no insurance. No money. Nothing.

The next day, going back to the burned-down house left in a pile of rubble was hard, but as we were driving up I saw something blue sur-rounded by all the black-and-grey embers and twisted metal. I wondered what it was and, as we got closer, I realized it was one of my favourite statues. It was a statue of the Blessed Virgin Mary. It was cracked, but not broken apart, just sitting on one of the timbers, still a vibrant blue. To me that was a massive sign from above that everything was going to be okay.

We had to stay at a friend's place, and what was really cool was how the town of Lodgepole responded. It was the closest town to us, a twenty-five-minute drive away, with a population of two hundred people. Within twenty-four hours, we had five truckloads of stuff brought to the place where we were staying. Clothes, money, household items, and fur-niture; you name it—people just gave. At that time, I hadn't even heard of the town of Okotoks [a ranching town south of Calgary, about an hour away from Lodgepole]. We received three boxes from people in Okotoks who had heard what had happened. We didn't even know them.

The way people pulled together had a lasting impact on me.

Two weeks later, my husband and I separated. So now, I was a single mom without a job and without an income. We had a tough time, the kids and I, trying to make it. Living in a large farming family taught me how to stretch a dollar and make good healthy food out of very little. We survived on homemade soup for quite a while.

There was a huge love between the girls and me, so incredibly strong. I remember us dancing in the living room of this trailer we lived in. We really had nothing, but I never felt as happy, even in a tough time. We had a richness within us. It's kind of hard to explain. We really didn't have anything, and it didn't matter. Perhaps through the lack, we found the abundance.

In the spring of 1993, we moved to Cochrane, where I got a job and started to rebuild our lives. It was a hard time, but a happy time. A fresh start. Something new. I met Ken and we've been happily married for fifteen years. The girls have all grown up to become truly unique people, and have since left home to follow their own lives. They are survivors.

It was really different and difficult when the girls left home and Ken and I became empty nesters. I had never been without kids. Right from when I was little, I spent time nurturing kids. So, when they all left, there was a huge void. It was really strange. I'd lived my life so much for kids that I really felt lost. I always told my children that the most rewarding job in the whole wide world was to be a parent. That's still my personal belief, as I'm sure it is for most parents.

So, over the next while, missing having children in my life was building to the point where all of a sudden, one day, I had this idea. I thought, "I want to do something for kids, and I want to involve my horses, because horses have done so much for me." I've seen what they have done for other people, as well. For example, I had a good friend who was dying of lung cancer. He was in pain all of the time. He would call me in the middle of the day and say, "Do you want to go for a ride?" and I would say, "Yup!" We'd trailer up, and off to the mountains we'd go. He could barely lift that saddle, but he didn't want me to help him with that or anything. He would say to me, "I have so much pain. But the minute I get on my horse, my pain disappears." Every time we would ride his "favourite" ride to the top of a particular mountain, he'd say to me, "Remember, Martha, when I go, this is where I want my ashes to be spread." My friend Lona and I granted his wish.

I worked as a Head Counsellor and Riding Leader for a kids' horse camp at the Bates Bar J Ranch. Seeing the power of the connection between a horse and a child helped me in my quest to involve the horses in my journey for kids. In February 2007, I decided I would do some sort of a ride to raise money for challenged children. My godson is a special needs child who has Opitz C Syndrome, which is very rare. He is non-verbal, cannot chew, has some mental ability challenges, and suffers seizures. This also strengthened my desire. So, thinking really big, I decided Alberta wasn't big enough; I thought I should do part of Canada. A couple of days later, I decided I would go from Ottawa to Calgary in the spring of 2008. I figured that would be about the amount of time I would have where the weather wouldn't be too cold or too hot for the horses. I had figured out the total kilometres and roughly how long it would take. The reason I chose Ottawa was that the national office for the Children's Wish Foundation is there. As well, I felt that our national capital would be a fitting place to begin.

At this point, I hadn't told anyone about my dream and then, three days later, my husband came home with this book he bought for me, *Ride the Rising Winds* by Barbara Kingscote. She had written about her ride on horseback across Canada back in the 1940s. Well, I almost keeled over, because he had no idea what was going on in my head. I said, "Thank you," and I grabbed the book. Right around the time he bought the book for me, I was trying to think about how many kilometres I could do in a day. I just opened the book randomly, and my eyes went directly to a sentence that read: "… her horse had given her consistently 30 miles a day and sometimes 50 miles a day." That was it. I closed the book and, the next day, I called Lona to tell her about my dream, even before telling my husband.

A few days later, I sat Ken down and told him I had made up my mind about something, and that there was no changing it. I was going to do it. I think I scared him a bit, but he sat down and, after listening to me, he agreed to support me. It really started from there, though there were a lot of barriers along the way. I never saw them as barriers at the time; I just saw them as challenging roadblocks that I had to divert around.

My father, John Vandelaar, passed away in July 2007, as I was planning my ride. I was very close to him. When I told my parents about my plan, my mother, Mary Vandelaar, was very skeptical, while my father was wide-eyed and excited. From one dreamer to another, he knew that I would do it. He ended up dying suddenly before the ride. That was really sad, because I knew he was going to be so proud of me. When he died, I had this force in me. I swear he was pushing me. I sure miss Dad.

And so the monumental task of planning started. At one point, Lona, who was helping to plan this whole thing, said to me, "You know this has gotten really big. We haven't told many people yet, so if you want to back out, we can." I said, "I will do this. Come hell or high water, I will do this." She just smiled and, together, we dug in our heels. We soon realized that we needed help and formed a committee of fifteen dedicated volunteers.

It took a year to plan the ride, and it took on a life of its own. I was just on a roll for that year. I got really focused, and there wasn't a lot that could pull me away. My kids were very supportive, yet seeing their mother work tirelessly around the clock and anticipating the safety issues of the whole event worried them. I was pushing so hard that I couldn't see their concern at the time, because I was just so committed to helping all these other kids. In the long run, the ride and the commitment has now become a good example for my kids, and they are proud of their mom.

A few times I was asked if I questioned my decision to take on this endeavour. I didn't experience that until two weeks into the ride. That was the first time I wondered, "What the heck have I gotten myself into?" I knew, from growing up on the farm, that you hoe one row at a time. You just look at that one row and you don't look at all the other rows; otherwise, you'd want to sit down and cry. I took this learning and experience with me and handled my ride in this same way. I would always just look at the day at hand. If I ever looked at the map (which I did at the end of every day to see the accomplishment in distance for that day), I would never look beyond the day. I knew that I could accomplish it one day at a time.

I left Ottawa with four horses (Coco, Daisy, Rapper, and Champagne) on March 30, 2008, in a temperature of minus-thirty degrees. The horses picked up a trot from the time they left till the time they arrived home. Six weeks of the ride had snow, so the strain on the body and the spirit, at times, definitely wore on me. Two weeks into the ride, I had had a very emotional day, meeting a lot of "wish" children and their families in Espanola, Ontario. At the end of that day's ride, at an organized meet-and-greet, I went back to the trailer emotionally and physically exhausted. I looked at my map and saw how far I had come—about sixty kilometres between two horses, Coco and then Daisy. Then I made the mistake of looking at the rest of the distance to see how far I had yet to go—about 3,750 kilometres! It was like all the air went out of my balloons. I laid on my bed thinking, "What have I done?" and just really prayed about it. I knew I had to keep going. I knew there was no way I was going to quit, but I needed strength. I fell asleep praying and, when I woke up in the morning, I felt like a freight train. There was nothing that was going to stop me. I just felt empowered.

I woke up and thought, "Wow, look at me. I feel so strong." During the rest of the ride, the experience was more than I could have imagined, meeting so many "wish" children and their families and so many beautiful, caring people along the way. Every night, I was in a different place and, thanks to the hard work of the Bearspaw Lions Club and the eighty-plus Lions Clubs along the way, it was well-organized at every stop.

We initially thought about asking the Bearspaw Lions Club of Calgary for a donation to help with the expenses, which were going to be pretty huge. Lona asked her husband, Hopeton Louden, who is a member of the Lions Club, if we could go to one of their meetings to pitch our story. We had estimated that the expenses would be just over $50,000 and were hoping they would give us a donation for however much money they could. Instead, they ended up embracing the whole idea and agreed to do so much more. They came back to us saying, "You know what? We'd like to sponsor you. We're going to book every night along the way and donate a large sum of money to take care of the fuel, food, and a donation as well." And they did. That was huge. They contacted all the Lions Clubs along my route. What a gift. They made sure the horses had feed and water. The schedule was tight. I had to make sure I was there at the right time each night, because there were barbecues and pancake breakfasts that the Lions and the Children's Wish Foundation had organized. They hosted some big events.

I think one of the reasons the Lions got behind this adventure was that there were some horse people in the Lions Club, and maybe they thought, "Wow, this little five-foot-one gal is going to ride across most of Canada?" I think the other reason the Lions Club got behind this ride is that it had to do with kids. Lions are big-hearted people who have a strong commitment to helping the needy, especially the children. Some of the other big sponsors that enabled the ride to happen were Cochrane Dodge, with the donation of a one-ton dually truck; Bar T5 Trailers, with the donation of a four-horse gooseneck horse trailer; and Garmin, for the donation of the navigation equipment. The ride couldn't have happened without all of these people.

I spoke to kids at schools, spoke to Lions Clubs, and did media interviews. I made lots of speeches. Every night, somebody else put us up with our horses and our trailers. I met so many people. People along the way were stopping to give donations, whether it was a pail of water alongside the road for the horses, a bag of apples, farrier and vet services, food, money, etc. I've always said that Canada is full of such beautiful people. And what I found throughout this ride is that, when people give from the heart, it spreads like throwing a stone in calm waters. It just ripples and ripples and ripples.

Everybody jumped on in so many ways. There were kids coming out and giving everything they had in their piggy banks. One little girl came up to me and gave me her marble—she learned the value of "losing her marbles" at a young age, didn't she?—and said, "I don't have any money, but this is my favourite marble." There was a boy who had received a wish from the Children's Wish Foundation and was in a wheelchair. He had had a horrible go in life and wanted to give me a donation of one of his little puppies. I named that puppy to remember this kind, young boy facing his own life challenges. I still have that puppy today. His name is Chance. One couple gave the money that they received in gifts from their wedding and also donated the money that they would have spent on gifts for the guests to Giddy Up for Wishes.

What I found is that people wanted to experience what I was experiencing through their giving. They really did. There were some people who rode along with me when I came into their area. A couple of hours, a half-day, or a full day—they shared the experience. My volunteer drivers and road crew thought they were going to be bored to tears driving on the side of the road at ten to fifteen kilometres an hour. They brought books and never once opened them. The experience was not anything they could have imagined. Every week, I had new drivers. My husband, Ken, and my nephew, Francois, drove for the week that took me out of Ontario and into Manitoba, a monumental accomplishment, as it took me seven weeks to get out of Ontario with very rough terrain. The wide-open spaces and shoulders were a welcome sight for the horses and me. I had great involvement from family members and friends. Their comments were simple: "Wow!" "Amazing!"

The ride was completed on our return to Cochrane on July 1 for the Canada Day Celebrations. We'd raised approximately $210,000 for the Children's Wish Foundation. The experience has given me more faith in mankind than I ever had before. The ride brought out the good in absolutely everybody. I never met a negative person. The media got people excited, and it was unbelievable how everybody fell in love with the whole idea. Canadians are beautiful people, and I am proud to say that I met many of them along the Trans-Canada Highway.

Hal and Dana asked me what my definition of a life worth living might be now, having completed this tremendous life adventure. If I have to describe a life worth living, it would be living a life rich in love and happiness. It is in the giving that we receive. Giving to others, especially those in need, is so very rewarding. It's a win-win for all. I feel that a person lives by example. If you live from the heart, you can find true worth in everything. If you see your world in colour, life is fuller. A lot of people go through life and never see the colour. Just let it start with you. Others will catch on and join you.

I say be fearless. Live lively. Don't let anybody tell you that you can't do something. See everything as a possibility, and don't let fear get in the way. Dream big, and don't be afraid, because we live in a society where sometimes dreamers are ridiculed. Be like a child. Give yourself permission to have your head in the clouds. Children dream in full colour; they think they can do anything. Don't lose that child within you, because children dream and laugh from the bottom of their toes. They laugh at everything. The other day, my grandson was laughing and laughing over nothing. Then I found myself laughing and we were both hysterical. I have no idea what we were laughing about! You've all experienced that at one point in your lives. Don't lose that! Don't wait for a child to get you laughing hysterically about nothing at all. It's in this state that we forget all the stressors in our lives and just let our hearts sing through laughter.

When we go through life, it can be really tough for a lot of people at times. Everybody's busy trying to make money and just busy with life, but if they could just say, "Whoa, stop the horse," they could see the colours rather than everything zooming by in black and white. My biggest message on my ride was to dream. If I could give those kids going through chemo or other challenges hopes and dreams, I slept well that night. And I'm happy to say that I witnessed this many times. I've often said that the smile on the face of a child and the sound of their giggle are two of the most beautiful things to witness. Like seven year-old Emily, giggling uncontrollably while sitting on the back of a horse (Coco) for the first time. Her parents informed me the next day that Emily hadn't smiled once in the six months prior to this while going through her chemo treatments. That was very fulfilling. That's how I want to be remembered, giving kids hope and permission to keep dreaming in colour.

Now that the ride is over and the experience is part of my past, I can still feel the effects of it all. It altered my life in ways that are hard to explain.

A person needs to create their own "peak experience" to understand the tremendous impact it can have on their life. Giving of a person's time and money to a charity is admirable, but there is an opportunity for all of us to create an experience that takes us out of our comfort zones and the everyday humdrum of life. Live life on the edge. Push out. You'll find a life even more worth living. ∎

SO NOW WHAT?

Martha encourages us to give ourselves permission to have our head in the clouds, to dream in full colour like a child. Her description of both her and her grandson laughing hysterically over apparently nothing speaks to the simplicity and purity of a child's worldview. Her grandson was obviously experiencing something from within that was causing him to laugh uncontrollably. Emily, who sat briefly on Martha's horse during the trip, began to laugh uncontrollably and experience the moment. It just happens—unintended, unexpected, and joyful. As Martha pointed out, most of us have experienced this type of feeling in our lives. It seems to come out of nowhere and it stirs deep emotions.

Connecting with those unintended, unexpected feelings or moments in our lives can be a stepping stone to creating our own peak experience. Martha wants to be remembered for giving kids hope and permission to keep dreaming in colour. John Davidson has hitched his peak experiences to raising awareness of Duchenne muscular dystrophy as well as creating an endowment to help find a cure. As you encounter the other individuals interviewed for this book, you will discover that each of them has some cause close to their heart that pulled them forward.

- Is there a cause that touches your heart that could lead you into a peak experience of your own? What is it? Why is it important to you?

- How could you create a peak experience that would take you out of your Comfort Zone to help that cause in some small way?

- What one or two steps can you take now or in the near future to begin exploring this potential peak experience? When can you start?

- What marbles will you most likely need to use: Time, Talent, or Treasure?

CHAPTER FIVE

PEAK EXPERIENCES IN THE LIFEWORTH ZONE

What lies behind us and what lies before us are
tiny matters compared to what lies within us.

RALPH WALDO EMERSON

In the Introduction, we defined *Lifeworth* as living a life worth living for yourself and/or for others. It occurs when individuals, at various times in their lives, discover purpose and meaning, creativity and vitality. John Davidson provided us with another great definition: "A life worth living is a life that lets you fall asleep quickly and comfortably, knowing that you're doing that which you fully and truly believe you are here to do."

We have connected the concept of *Lifeworth* to the Comfort Zone by creating a new zone called the Lifeworth Zone. The Lifeworth Zone, as depicted in Figure 5.1, is the area where we find opportunities to identify and satisfy our inner yearnings for *Lifeworth,* for our personal peak experiences, or for helping others in a significant way. We have separated the Comfort Zone from the Lifeworth Zone by something we call "the wall."

The wall refers to the psychological and/or physical barriers that can keep us from experiencing a more fulfilling life beyond the Comfort Zone. It can be an imposing and daunting obstacle, making it quite difficult for many individuals to venture into the Lifeworth Zone. We will explore the concept of the wall in more detail in Chapter 9.

Figure 5.1

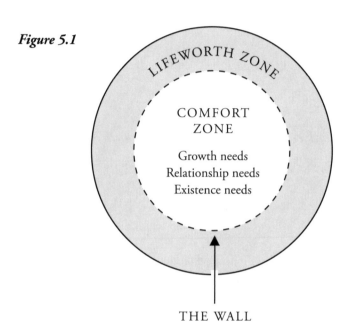

THE WALL

The Lifeworth Zone contains special types of experiences that occur outside of the Comfort Zone. Like the Comfort Zone, the Lifeworth Zone involves personal development and growth. However, the feelings that occur in the Lifeworth Zone differ from those generally experienced in the Comfort Zone. So much of what we do in the Comfort Zone can be quite ordinary, aimed primarily at maintaining our Comfort Zone at a desired level of satisfaction. The Lifeworth Zone contains experiences that are precious moments of highest happiness or joy, or of deepest sorrow and pain. They can involve sudden feelings of intense happiness, well-being, wonder, awe, or sorrow. They are personally valued experiences of such significance that they stand out in our minds in more or less permanent contrast to the experiences of everyday life. These experiences can change the course of our lives and are intrinsically rewarding. They tend to expand our Comfort Zone, creating a desire for new experiences and making it difficult to go back to the way things were before the experience. We refer to these experiences in the Lifeworth Zone as "peak experiences."

Lifeworth can be about creating or living through peak experiences for you personally. These experiences have an inward focus and are more about looking inside ourselves and asking questions such as: What am I doing for myself? If I am not doing things for myself, what am I missing (e.g., spirituality, adventure, helping others, learning a new skill)? Am I getting my own life's worth? Am I doing what I was meant to do? Am I pursuing or exploring things that I am interested in, or that challenge me? These types of experiences could be anything from rafting through a river canyon, travelling through the history of Europe, attending a concert of your favourite group of musicians, learning to speak a different language, developing new woodworking skills, or learning how to write poetry. The list can be endless. These experiences are defining moments that have a profound impact on the way you live your life.

Lifeworth may also mean focusing on efforts to help others meet their needs, on making a difference in the lives of other people. These experiences are usually outward focused and are more about looking outside of ourselves, where we ask questions such as: What legacy or footprint will I leave in the world? What is my life worth to my family, to my community, to society? Am I achieving my life's purpose? This can mean giving of one's Time, Talent, and/or Treasure Marbles in a significant, sustainable, and meaningful way in order to make the world a better place.

All of the people interviewed for this book had something deeper that was pulling them forward. As well, it appears that they all found ways to use their peak experiences to help others. As you will see from their stories, sometimes both types of peak experiences (inward and outward focused) were contained within one experience. In other cases, one type of experience led to the other.

Peak experiences are the gateways that take us from our Comfort Zone, through the wall, and into our Lifeworth Zone. They help us break the bonds of our Comfort Zone and experience life at deeper, more meaningful, rewarding levels.

So, just what are peak experiences? What do they look like? How do they feel? How would you recognize one? Is there a standard definition? Are they open to individual interpretation? We would like to share nine characteristics of peak experiences that we have identified and how they relate to the people we interviewed. They are life purpose, internal cues, uniqueness, time, multiplicity, risk and fear, limit-stretching, determination, and emotions. These characteristics will help you recognize peak experiences that you may have already experienced in your life and help you define new peak experiences in your future. Let's explore each one briefly.

Peak experiences involve being able to be what we are, to do what we are capable of doing, to recognize and achieve part of our life's purpose outside of our Comfort Zone. We see ourselves as learning from the experience and becoming energized as a fuller, more differentiated, more competent human being. Peak experiences can occur when life is being lived at its fullest in the moment, when the experience has been perspective-altering, or when there is a sense of being a part of something bigger. Through these peak experiences, we feel a greater sense of wholeness and fullness as a human being. We all have a desire to discover and live our life's purpose. We want to be who we were meant to be and do what we were meant to do. Certainly, we begin to accomplish this in the Growth needs area inside the Comfort Zone. We pursue careers and interests and develop skills and abilities that are relevant and meaningful to us in our early years. But it is peak experiences that actually expand on the growth in the Comfort Zone. They help us more fully realize our deeper yearnings, our personal potential, and our individual fulfillment.

Some individuals are able to discover their passions earlier than others. Lindsay Sears (Chapter 8) started barrel racing at an early age and was a world champion at twenty-seven. Paul Henderson (Chapter 12) pursued his love of hockey at an even earlier age and lived his passion for eighteen seasons in the NHL and WHA. Some discover their passions later in life. John Davidson left his successful career as a broadcaster to pursue his dream, with his son Jesse, of finding a cure for Duchenne muscular dystrophy. Martha Birkett was a young grandmother when she set out riding her horse from Ontario to Alberta for the Children's Wish Foundation.

Pursuing peak experiences in the Lifeworth Zone involves recognizing internal cues from our abilities, achievements, and experiences. These cues do not rely on other people; they come from within and are a signal that there is something deep within us causing the feeling. You may walk into a bookstore and, on the surface, feel a sense of belonging or happiness. Being surrounded by rows and rows of books and the fresh smell of paper and ink just seems to fit with who you are. The deeper prodding you sense could be an innate desire to write a novel or develop a rare book collection, which you have not had time to explore. In another example, you may walk into a hospital to visit a friend and feel a sense of belonging or comfort come over you. It may stir a long-buried desire to volunteer in some type of health-care setting to help others in need. While standing in the hospital emergency room as the doctors fought in vain to save her husband, Katy Hutchison (Chapter 11) had an "aha" moment, a moment when she felt "a wash of emotion and light flood over me. I had a real sense of having to choose who I was going to be." As you will discover, Katy listened and acted on that internal cue.

Peak experiences are highly unique and individual in nature: success at sports or tests of physical endurance, intense feelings of love, exposure to great music or art, the overwhelming beauty of nature, or a feeling of oneness with a higher power. You can physically participate in the experience (e.g., running your first marathon, winning a sporting competition, jamming on stage with your favourite blues artist), or you can participate as an observer (e.g., feeling the vibrations of a great concert moving through your body, or watching your children explore an endless beach, looking for starfish left by the outgoing tide in the warm afternoon sun).

Peak experiences are unique to each of us because we perceive them on an individual basis. Even though we may be achieving a peak experience with other people at the same time, the experience is individual in nature. All of the runners in a marathon will come away with their own unique peak experience. We filter our peak experiences through our particular perceptions of the world. Two people can experience similar events yet undergo very different changes as a result. John Davidson and Martha Birkett travelled across parts of Canada on some of the same highways—one on foot, one on horseback. Their journeys were ones of immense hope and support for important causes. Although the events were similar in some ways, the experiences of each person were unique to them in ways that only they could appreciate and remember.

James Carse, in his book *Breakfast at the Victory*, provides a great parable that symbolizes the impact of perception on people experiencing the same event.

One morning, the master said to his students that they would walk to the top of the mountain. The students were surprised because even those who had been with him for years thought the master was oblivious to the mountain whose crest looked serenely on their town.

By midday, it became apparent that the master had lost direction. Moreover, no provision had been made for food. There was increasing grumbling, but he continued walking, sometimes through underbrush and sometimes across faces of crumbling rock. When they reached the summit in the late afternoon, they found other wanderers already there who had strolled up a well-worn path. When the students complained to the master, he said only, "These others had climbed a different mountain."

Both Martha and John, while covering similar sections of the Trans-Canada Highway, had "climbed different mountains." Each person in this book has climbed his or her own mountain, even if others have done something similar, either before or after them. Katy Hutchison is not the first woman to lose a husband and use that experience to make a difference in the lives of others. She just climbed her own mountain in her own way. Alan Hobson (Chapter 14) was not the first, nor the last to climb Mount Everest. He climbed it in his own way with his team and his experience has led him to more personal mountains to climb. There are two points here. The first is that you don't have to completely reinvent a peak experience to create your own. You can build on, modify, or adapt the peak experiences and inspiration of others. The second point is that it is your perception of your peak experience and the impact it has on your life and the lives of others that is important.

Time is another characteristic of peak experiences and we believe they are impacted by three different elements of time. First, peak experiences can take place over different lengths of time. The experience can be very brief, as it was for Paul Henderson when he scored the series-winning goal during the 1972 Canada-Soviet hockey series; or for Lindsay Sears each time she settles into her well-worn saddle on her horse Martha to run the barrels. Success and peak experiences at this level can be measured in one-hundredths of a second. Or the experiences can be longer, like the four months Martha Birkett endured riding a horse across Canada for the Children's Wish Foundation (and that doesn't include her months of planning the ride); or even lengthier, like Alan Hobson's three attempts over several years to accomplish his life goal of summiting Mount Everest. Second, peak experiences can occur at different times over the course of our lives. We can experience them in childhood, during our early adult years, during those middle-age years when we begin to ask ourselves *Lifeworth* types of questions, and even in our senior years when we have time to reflect on our lives. Peak experiences can occur at any time in our lives using the resources and marbles we have in our marble bag at that time. Third, peak experiences can be planned or unplanned, deliberate or unexpected. Like Martha, we can plan to ride across part of Canada and we can achieve it. However, also like Martha, we do not expect a house fire that claims all of our belongings. Both are peak experiences, one anticipated, one not. Like Katy Hutchison, we can do nothing to prepare for the murder of a spouse, but we can plan to turn that one peak experience into another one. Like Alan Hobson, we can do nothing to prepare for a diagnosis of cancer, but we can plan to turn that experience into peak experiences of helping others climb back from cancer.

There is a sense of multiplicity about peak experiences. We can and will experience a large number of them in various forms during our lifetime. They are not an "end" goal, not a one-goal phenomenon, not one-time events. Peak experiences are transient by nature. They do not and cannot last indefinitely. Intense periods of emotions of most types are episodic, not continuous in nature. We can move in and out of the Lifeworth Zone many times over the course of our lives through different peak experiences, some planned, some totally unexpected. After each peak experience, we will naturally return to our Comfort Zone, which will have been changed in some way by the experience. The ups and downs on the path to peak experiences are part of the natural course. Each experience sets the bar higher or creates a need or desire for another or different peak experience. Abraham Maslow, the well-known psychologist who gave us the theory of the Hierarchy of Needs, calls this the "Grumble Theory." The Grumble Theory simply states that satisfying certain needs only leads to temporary happiness, which, in turn, tends to be succeeded by another (hopefully) higher yearning for another peak experience. This is one way that we can grow and expand our Comfort Zone during our lifetime.

Many, if not most, peak experiences involve elements of risk and/or fear. It is the sense of risk that causes us to stretch out of our Comfort Zone, to expand our capabilities and confidence. Once we reach new limits, it is no longer okay to say, "I don't think I can do it," or "What if I fail?" There were high levels of risk when Alan Hobson and his team made an unsuccessful first attempt to summit Mount Everest. They expanded their limits and experience on that first attempt. When they attempted to reach the summit a second and a third time, their boundaries of risk, experience, and knowledge expanded. Alan and his team finally converted all of this experience into a successful summit of Everest.

The other side of risk is the level of fear it can create in our minds. When Tom Droog (Chapter 6) started sunflower-seed giant Spitz International, he was entering completely new territory. In the early years, there was always the risk of losing everything he and his wife, Emmy, had built. The fear generated by risk can be substantial, and it can become a barrier to action. In Tom's words, "I believe it is fear that holds back so many of us from truly following our dreams. Whether it is fear of trying something new or fear of letting go of something old, we all have a fear of failing or a fear of succeeding." We will talk more about fear and risk in Chapter 10.

The desire to stretch our skills and abilities to new limits and to develop or learn new skills during the experience is key to a peak experience. The level of skill or talent required to accomplish a peak experience can affect its success and our satisfaction. Peak experiences can be perceived as almost insurmountable or impossible if our skill level or talents are not in the range of abilities required to at least try an activity. For example, as an avid hiker, Dana has hiked for many years in the Canadian Rockies, including challenging scramble climbs, but he had never experienced being tethered on the end of a rope slowly working his way up a rock face on the side of a mountain. Dana first learned to climb with his son Jeff on indoor climbing walls when he was in his mid-fifties—definitely a Comfort Zone-stretching experience. With enough practice, his skills improved and he eventually headed out to climb on real rock faces. The first time he climbed a short rock face with his son was definitely a peak experience. Part of the peak experience was developing those skills during the experience itself. Dana's skill level and confidence increased on subsequent short climbs. When he and Jeff attempted a multi-pitch, longer climb by staying on a 400-foot rock face for a few hours, the climb became another peak experience that required the combination of the skills learned on the basic climbs as well as new skills gained on this tougher climb. Peak experiences help us build on and expand the skills we have as well as help us learn entirely new skills.

Our level of determination also affects our peak experiences. While lack of determination can keep us from achieving a peak experience in the first place, strong determination, coupled with intense emotion, can compensate for skills that are merely adequate or sufficient at the time. We will learn the skills we need during the peak experience because we are determined to be successful in the moment. This is what occurred for Dana in his rock-climbing experience as he graduated from short to longer climbs of increasing difficulty. Dana is also a long-time student of the martial arts, having practised traditional Fudokan-Shotokan karate for over thirty years. As a third-degree black belt (*San Dan*), he continues to be active in karate as both a student and a *sensei* (teacher). With respect to determination, Dana teaches his karate students that a strong spirit (*kihaku*) will always bolster techniques that are not quite at the level they should be. The students come to understand that excellence in karate is a quest for perfection that continues to pull them forward to higher skill levels. Spirit and determination are key to achieving a peak experience and shifting the balance toward a successful experience.

Emotions are a key portal through which we experience many events in our lives. They are also one of the critical drivers behind our behaviours and experiences. We can experience the awe and wonder of our children being born, or the sorrow and pain of losing someone close to us. Both are peak experiences, both are life-changing events, and both involve very high levels of emotion. The difference is the type of emotion: joy or sorrow. The emotions can be very positive or, for lack of a better word, very negative. The higher the level of emotion experienced, the more indelible the experience. We can continue to experience some levels of the emotions several years after the related event has occurred. Think of a time when you achieved one of your more difficult goals, were on a winning team, delivered your first speech, held your first child, experienced your first heartache. Can you remember the satisfaction, enjoyment, excitement, sorrow, or sadness you felt at the time? If you have lost someone close to you, can you still feel the lingering sadness in having lost them, or the joy and fulfillment of having known them?

The Lifeworth Zone moves with us throughout our lives. Sometimes, it is close and attainable; at other times, it is distant and seemingly unachievable. Getting into the Lifeworth Zone often involves an element of risk. But—and this is a big but—the good news is that we can move in and out of this zone, in our own unique way, using the life marbles we have in our bag at that point in time. It fully depends on how we define peak experiences for ourselves. We try to match the capacity and resources of our lives to the costs of achieving a particular peak experience. If we try to attain a peak experience that is too far beyond the capacity of our marble bag at that time, we might be setting ourselves up for frustration or disappointment. If we try to achieve a peak experience well within our grasp and the capacity of our marble bag, well within our Comfort Zone, there may be some question as to whether or not it is truly a peak experience. Remember, a peak experience is one that stretches and grows your capacity as a human being. It is one that causes your Comfort Zone to expand, by even the smallest degree. ■

SO NOW WHAT?

We have now added the Lifeworth Zone to our model. This is a zone just outside the Comfort Zone and is separated from the Comfort Zone by the wall. The wall is a psychological wall, sometimes of Herculean proportions, that keeps us trapped in our Comfort Zone. You have also learned that peak experiences are the pathways that appear at different points in our lives that can lead us from the Comfort Zone into the Lifeworth Zone.

- Take some time to reflect on your life. What types of past experiences have taken you out of your Comfort Zone and into the Lifeworth Zone?

- Which ones were positive experiences? Which ones negative?

- What impact did they have on you? How did you grow and develop as a result?

- Looking forward, what types of peak experiences could you create for yourself? Can you build on some of your past peak experiences to create a new one?

CHAPTER SIX

SPITZ CRACKED WIDE OPEN

—TOM DROOG

He who is not courageous enough to take risks will accomplish very little in life.

MUHAMMAD ALI

In 1970, at age twenty-two, Tom Droog decided to leave Holland, where he was born, to explore Canada. He was one of a group of young men who decided to make Canada their next life adventure. Most of them ended up settling in Ontario and other parts of Eastern Canada, but something about the West was calling Tom. He wanted to check out what he had heard about the wide-open spaces of the Canadian prairies. Once Tom saw the country around Bow Island, in southeastern Alberta, he was hooked.

Tom worked as a farmhand for the next four years, slowly learning the trade and, in 1974, with the help of a 95 percent government-backed loan, he purchased his first quarter section of land (160 acres or 65 hectares). Tom mastered the art of farming, but soon realized that he did not want to be left at the mercy of the Canadian Wheat Board, dictating what he could sell and for how much. Following a ten-day farm tour to the United States, he saw that farmers there were having good success growing sunflowers and selling the seeds, usually as bird feed. In 1978, Tom made a calculated gamble and started growing sunflower seeds, establishing a company called Spitz. Over the next three decades, he grew Spitz into an international empire and Spitz Sunflower Seeds became one of the most popular snacks in Canada and the U.S. In 2008, Tom sold Spitz to PepsiCo.

In 2010, Tom's wife and business confidant, Emmy, lost her three-year battle with cancer. For decades, they had been perfect for each other, in business and in marriage. As Tom describes her, Emmy was quiet, conservatively grounded, and treasured her family and her privacy. She also had a keen sense of what was "enough."

Although a driven businessman, Tom has a history of giving back to the community, both at home and around the world. He also has a passion for helping youth. He would be the first to acknowledge his good fortune, but he is paying it back and paying it forward. Here is Tom in his own words.

●　　●　　●　　●

Moving to Canada to start my adult life was my second-best decision. Marrying Emmy was my best. We met in Ontario when we were basically kids. There was something about Emmy that I still can't describe. She was the love of my life, my business partner, my grounding rod. Together, we made an incredible team, and I'm so happy Emmy lived to see Spitz grow into a North American player, with eighty employees supplying 75 percent of the Canadian sunflower seed market, and becoming the Number 3 brand in the U.S.

Like most people, we had a few ups and downs in life, but our marriage was always rock-solid. One of the high points in our lives was when Pepsi sent their corporate Lear jet with two private pilots to pick us up to finalize the sale of our life's work. Walking toward the jet—down the red carpet they had laid out for us with bouquets of sunflowers at the end— Emmy and I could hardly believe how far we had come. Starting out, we were two young Dutch kids, and now here we were boarding a private jet sent to pick us up. It was truly very emotional, and quite surreal. I feel blessed to have been so fortunate in business, and so very lucky to have Emmy say "yes" when I asked her to spend the rest of her life with me. I would never have had the successes in my life without Emmy. I miss her, but she is always with me. I can still feel her presence.

The road leading to where I am now at age sixty-two has sometimes been like the country roads I have travelled along all my life—full of smooth patches, often followed by washboard ruts and potholes. Some potholes have been huge, such as the time our two-and-a-half-year-old grandson Gabriel wandered off unnoticed on our farm and accidentally drowned in our dugout [a small pond holding water for use around the farm]. That was devastating for Emmy and me, but nowhere near as devastating as it was for our daughter, Christie, and our son-in-law, Oscar. A very tough time, which really changed our family forever. And, with God's help, we got up, refocused, reloaded, and started looking forward again in life.

Growing Spitz was a real adventure—one that I would do again—but there's an interesting story about how we decided to start growing sunflowers. For the first while, we had been growing flax. I was growing more and more frustrated as an entrepreneur, having a government agency, the Canadian Wheat Board, dictate how much I could sell, when, and for how much. That wasn't how I wanted to live my life and run our business. Flash ahead two years and, during a farm tour to the U.S., I saw farmers having a good run growing sunflowers. The market was wide open and not overrun with government intervention. So, in 1978, we started growing sunflowers.

It is interesting how the whole Spitz story started, as well. In 1979, we had been contracted to grow sunflowers for the United Grain Growers (UGG), which in turn sold it as bird feed. They were paying us ten cents a pound to supply them. But when I was visiting a friend near Okotoks, just outside of Calgary, she told me that she was paying thirty-eight cents a pound for her birdseed. That was one of those moments in my life where the light came on in my head. That's when I decided we should expand to include the cleaning of our own seed and then sell it retail for thirty-eight cents instead of ten cents to UGG. As we grew, we made the decision to start cleaning, roasting, and seasoning sunflower seeds and other seeds for human consumption. We jumped into the snack food market with both feet.

We had made plans to build a small cleaning facility right on our farm near Bow Island, Alberta, but, with some government encouragement and a promise for special farm financial assistance, we decided to go for it and build a much bigger facility. We dove in, had the plans drawn up, and started construction. It was right about then that we had our first lesson in trusting that a verbal agreement isn't always rock-solid. The government official promising the financial assistance died without leaving a record of our conversations or agreements, leaving us twisting in the wind for the first time in our business lives. Emmy and I were scrambling to find alternative financing, but, you have to remember, this was the late seventies and, at that time in Canada, we had record double-digit inflation and interest rates. We were seeing financing rates in the high teens, and the economy was starting to turn south. Finding financing became a real challenge and, for the first time, we wondered if our business would make it through this crisis, or if we would have to fold. Those were very stressful times, but, with some hoop-jumping, we had a bank back us. With hard work, perseverance, and lots of praying, we saw the expansion through to completion. We were now in the sunflower seed-cleaning business.

Another difficult period was in 2004, when 95 percent of the sunflower crops being grown on contract by local farmers for Spitz were of an unacceptable quality. Poor weather conditions that year meant that the sunflower crops were only of animal-feed quality, nowhere near the quality standards Spitz had established, and to which our loyal customer following had grown accustomed. Because of the shortage of good-quality new seed crops, we made the very risky decision to borrow $6 million to pay for the very best seeds from prior years, which now were much more expensive due to the new crop production shortages. We took a huge financial gamble, while our competitors decided to pay the lower prices for the lesser-quality new seeds. We were lucky. Our gamble paid off. Customers flocked to us in droves because our quality was so much better. We would later buy out those competitors who found themselves in trouble. We were very fortunate, because we stuck to our principles and to our standards of quality. Borrowing that much money, coupled with our now steep sales growth, put the financial squeeze on again. But, as we had learned to do in the past, we dug in, paid attention to the details, worked hard, and prayed—a lot.

Looking back at the great adventure of building Spitz into what it has become, I recall a number of times when Emmy and I were quite nervous and afraid about where the business was heading. But we were able to look fear straight in the eye and make the best business decision we could with the information we had at the time. I am now able to help others deal with their own fears because I believe that it is fear that holds back so many of us from truly following our dreams. Whether it is fear of trying something new or fear of letting go of something old, we all have a fear of failing or a fear of succeeding. Sometimes people don't believe they deserve something better in life. That's a shame. Why let fear cripple us? Why go to our graves wondering, "What if?"

I believe that if you do your research, you can make the best decisions possible and will be able to move forward in life in an exciting way. But you always have to be honest and truthful with yourself. I've always said, "The truth may hurt, but it will heal," because it took me years to face my fears. I have had a fear of failing. Not so much a fear of failing in business, but of failing Emmy. I never wanted to let her down. I never wanted her to have to go through a failure that I had created. Emmy helped me make some great decisions. Sometimes I wanted to grow faster. I wanted to get there faster and she would help me not get too far ahead of myself.

Together we helped each other build the company. Together we helped each other address our own fears of taking the next step or in pulling Spitz back from the brink. And through that we developed what we felt were the guiding principles for building a new business or taking a business to the next level. Here they are. Pretty simple, but very effective. They have served us well.

1. Keep your hands on the pulse of your business, but let your people make decisions. If you have good people around you, let them shine. Most people are smart and want to grow in their careers. Give them a chance. Share the power. Everyone wins.

2. Stay out of the e-mail trap. I see so many people, especially business owners, stuck in front of their computers or on their BlackBerries thinking they are working. In my view, give that job to someone else, stay more in touch with your business, be immersed *in* your business and not stuck working *on* your business. Quit sending your own e-mails and spend the time doing something more productive. Try it. You'll be amazed with the results by making that one small change.

3. Come up with a Number 1 quality product. At Spitz, we had just one focus—sunflower seeds—so we decided to do what we had to do to have the very best in quality. Think about what your main product or service is. If you have more than one, can you determine which one is the foundation of your business? Whatever your situation is, think

about what your customers want and what your competitors are doing. Is there an opportunity there? If you nail the quality and the focus, it goes straight to your bottom line.

4. Pay the highest prices in the industry. If you are in a business where you have to buy raw product, get the best raw product you can. With our contract farmers, we paid the most in the industry so that we could put a lock on the best production. Without good input, the output (final product) won't be there.

5. Pay your people well. You have heard many times from business owners that their staff is their most valuable asset. I can't emphasize that enough. Emmy and I steered the ship, but if we had not had good rowers, Spitz would not have become what it is. The true test of a business that is built from the bottom up is how well it can sustain that level of success when the owners are away, or in our case, when the business is sold. Spitz is still the leader in Canada and is even more successful now than when we sold it. That's because of our staff. We had some of the best employees anyone could hope for.

And finally, in addition to these basic principles, I always try to live my life with my faith in mind. I have a daily prayer routine that I make every effort to stick to. It helps keep me grounded and focused on what is truly important in life. It has helped me in business to remember that a deal has to be good for everyone—the seller, the buyer, and society.

Speaking about faith can make some people uncomfortable, but not me. The basic principles you will find embedded in your faith will help guide you through life if you give them a chance. Like the saying goes, "If you don't stand for something, you will fall for anything." I can't begin to tell you how it helped us get through some tough times in life—business challenges as well as the biggest challenge of all, Emmy's fight with cancer. I think it helped comfort her about what might be coming next. I know it helped me, and still does.

And through all the success, faith has helped me stay grounded and humble. Through all my blessings, my faith has helped me realize what my wealth really means and how I can help others with my good fortune. Hal and Dana asked me why I give so much and why I try to do it quietly. My answer is that there was this young, skinny Dutch kid who landed in Canada with barely enough for bus fare, and so many people gave him a "hand up." I never wanted nor received a "hand out."

So now my passion is to help others, especially the kids. I want to give kids with no chance an opportunity to get ahead. There are many youth in Canada who need help. That is why I have sponsored scholarships in numerous colleges and universities. The gift and support doesn't have to be big. People with any means can help if they really want to.

Outside of Canada, there is also a huge void in support and financial aid for children living in less fortunate countries. We can do so much with so little and accomplish so much in these countries. You don't have to be wealthy to really make a difference. Many years ago, a friend of mine was helping build orphanages in Guatemala and he asked if I wanted to go. It sparked my interest, so I went along. It changed my life. I realized then how truly blessed we are to live in Canada and how fortunate I was personally. I had this feeling that this might be one of the things I was called to do. We search throughout our lives for the meaning of life and to discover what our purpose might be. Going on that first trip pushed me in the right direction.

The orphanage is called Friends of the Orphans Canada, and we now have orphanages in Guatemala, Honduras, Mexico, and Peru. We started with one building and then decided to raise enough to build the whole orphanage. We kept expanding to other countries to what we have today.

I spend two weeks a year helping to construct the orphanages and to build these facilities. I have been asked how it makes me feel to be involved there. All I can say is that it warms me inside to see these kids getting an education they otherwise wouldn't have received and to have a chance to develop into the person they hoped they could be, to create a life for themselves, to bring some value to their community.

So much can be done with so little. In Guatemala, we helped Julia get though primary school and then I personally financed two years of college and helped her start a small Internet café in her village. I also helped her with the struggles any new business owner faces in getting started. I sent someone down there to help her deal with issues and people. I didn't want her to fail just because she didn't initially have the skill sets needed to deal with these start-up issues. She needed something more than money, and today her business is doing well. That helps me sleep at night. Someone helped me get started. I feel I need to pay back society.

But a word of caution with gifting: I realized that I had to be careful with how much and in what manner I give. Just throwing money at something can have negative consequences. I remember a time in Peru where we had hired five boys from the orphanage to help out with some of the construction. At the end, I gave each of them ten dollars. That is not a lot of money to you or me, but to them, it was an enormous sum. So much so, that two of the boys left the orphanage thinking they had it made. But the rule in the orphanage is that if you leave, you can't come back. Man, I had to do some talking and dancing to help those boys get back in the orphanage. What a huge learning experience that was for me. I have carried that lesson with me into my gifting in Canada. The numbers might be different, but the same cautions have to be there as well.

I believe education is the key for youth, whether they live in Canada or any other country. Education brings the community to a higher level, where people can see possibilities they otherwise might not. I had an opportunity to go to school in Holland. After high school, I went to an agricultural school as well as a technical school, but I haven't really had the time to pursue other education since. Life has been very full, but now I find myself speaking at colleges and universities, helping kids think about their futures, to dream of possibilities and to face their fears. In addition to donating money to these institutions to help with scholarships, I think part of my paying-it-forward plan is to work with youth. Sure, giving money is very helpful, but like Julia in Guatemala, they also need help and guidance beyond the money. That's how we can all make a difference. You don't have to have a lot of money to make a difference. Donating your time and your talents is as important as donating your treasures.

Hal and Dana asked me for my definition of a life worth living. Mine is pretty simple—just love life and live it to the fullest. Like many people, I love other cultures. I love learning about their customs, their challenges, and what they might teach me about living my life. In this book, you will be learning about peak experiences that enrich our lives. Two of our most memorable peak experiences were when Emmy and I were recognized as top Entrepreneurs of the Year in Canada by the national law firm of Borden, Ladner, Gervais LLP. The other one was being recognized as one of the top fifty private companies in Canada.

For me, the Entrepreneur of the Year award was especially rewarding, because I really believe that there is a difference between being a business person and being an entrepreneur. Business people have the talent to manage people and processes. Entrepreneurs dream up the ideas and are willing to take the risks. You don't often see people being able to be both a good business person and an entrepreneur. I know I wasn't. Emmy was the business person. I was the one with all the ideas and schemes. Emmy's skill sets were such a great complement to mine.

Looking to the future, with Spitz sold and Emmy gone, I have wondered what my purpose is going forward. I think it's an extension of what

Emmy and I had been doing all along—helping the kids. I feel I have an obligation to continue to help them, but to help them in the right way—financially, physically, and emotionally.

I have always hoped that I will become what I was meant to be. Some people ask how I will know if I ever get there. Well, I don't know. All I can do is keep moving forward in life trusting that the right doors will be opened and that I will know which direction I should be going. I know that if it feels good deep in my gut, it's the right direction. I feel led when I'm working with children who need help in helping themselves, helping create a chance for those who have no chance.

If I live another fifteen or twenty years, I hope that my legacy will be that I motivated people to move on their ideas, to get off their butts and do something. If I can mentor young people to move forward in a positive and productive way in their lives, I will feel very satisfied with that as my legacy. ■

SO NOW WHAT?

Tom and Emmy created a successful financial venture through the growth and sale of Spitz International. However, Tom points out that "you don't have to have a lot of money to make a difference. Donating your time and talents is as important as donating your treasures."

To Tom, the important thing is to take action, any kind of action. When a friend mentioned the opportunity to help build an orphanage in Guatemala, he jumped at the chance and continues with that mission today.

He also wondered what his purpose was going forward and felt he would recognize his purpose because it "feels good deep in my gut." During his hard work to build Spitz and his efforts to support children, he has followed the doors that opened for him.

- Is there something that makes you feel good deep in your gut, something that gives you a sense of purpose at this point in your life? What doors are open for you? Perhaps it is something you have wanted to do since your childhood, since you started a new job, or since you retired.

- What marbles (resources) do you have in your marble bag right now that you could use toward creating a peak experience? Are there additional marbles you might need (Time, Talent, or Treasure)? If so, how will you get them?

- Once you define a peak experience for yourself, is there someone you could share it with? Is there someone who could also benefit from a shared peak experience?

CHAPTER SEVEN

FREE REINING

If you obey all the rules, you miss all the fun.

KATHARINE HEPBURN

F ree Reining is about dreaming of possibilities, wondering about life, and *making* the time to face our fears. All those who wander, are not lost. All those who wonder, are not confused. Where did the concept of Free Reining come from?

It was in one of those pre-dawn slumber states where Hal was sort of asleep. Many would argue that this state could apply to Hal at any time, day or night, but in this particular instance, it was a time when he was more or less aware of his thoughts. It was then that the concept of Free Reining came to him. He's not sure why it came to him, but he suspects it might have been because of a recent experience he had while riding horses in the Rockies. Let Hal describe this experience to you in his own words.

Picture in your mind's eye, a beautiful summer day in the Rocky Mountains southwest of Calgary, Alberta. It's been a hot, blue-sky day on the horses, retracing the Sheep River back to its origins, back to its head waters where the creeks drain down the gorges of some of the most magnificent mountains on Earth. The Rockies are larger than life, ageless sentries lining both sides of the valley. They are nature's catchers' mitts, standing tall, collecting the year-round moisture from the constantly changing seasons and weather patterns.

It is here that a person can witness nature at its finest, tricklers become creeks, creeks become streams, and streams become a river. It is here that a person can see nature's handiwork, the creation of two rivers, the Sheep River and the Elbow River: the Sheep travelling east, eventually passing through Okotoks, and the Elbow flowing northeast, eventually passing through Calgary.

It's been a long day in the saddle. It's late afternoon and we are heading east back to camp. The horses instinctively know they are going home so the pace has quickened. We are at that place where the Sheep River is still gathering, still a baby river running wide and shallow. I know this part of the trail well. It's an open valley trail with the Sheep River crossing in front of us, disappearing to the left and then reappearing, weaving right, repeating this pattern for quite a while. I know the river is a foot or so deep with only a bed of pebbles, no large rocks for the horses to stumble on. I have been there many times.

I am riding with three good friends: Bevin Leipert, Ryan Gibson, and Vern Trail from Moose Jaw, Saskatchewan. They are part of the Moose Jaw Shriners Riding Club on their way to ride in the Calgary Stampede parade. With the river crossing back and forth in front of us, we thought it would be fun to let the horses run.

But first, let's flash back to when I first met Vern about four years earlier. He was seventy-eight years young. We had met these same Saskatchewan friends in the Cypress Hills, which sit on the border between Alberta and Saskatchewan. Vern had been bucked off his horse the day before and had bruised a couple of his ribs. He didn't ride with us that day, but he certainly entertained us around the campfire that night. Cowboy (Vern's nickname) had story after story, joke after joke, and had us laughing and howling the whole night. I remember saying to one of my other brothers, Craig—my lifelong riding buddy—that I hoped I would be like Vern at that age, still full of adventure, humour, stories, and an inspiration to everyone around him.

Flash ahead and here we are in the Sheep River valley ready to open up the horses. Vern, now eighty-two, says, "I'm coming with you" (expletives deleted). All in one motion, we squeeze our legs, make a "clucking" sound, and shift our weight forward to create slack in the reins. The horses recognize the cues and drop their back ends down and instantly we launch into turbo speed. Vern and his horse are right there rocketing down this twisting, turning path, laughing as we go and then bam!—the Sheep River is crossing in front of us. We pound through it and then are back onto the twisting, turning path. Farther down, bam!—the Sheep is back again, crossing in front of us. This continues for what seems like an hour, but is really only a few minutes. Mistakenly concerned about my elderly friend, and not wanting to see him get hurt, I turn back in my saddle to check on Vern.

And that's when it happens—the most amazing thing I have ever witnessed on a horse. It was like someone switched everything into slow motion. Looking behind me to the west, the sun, in all its magnificence, is setting low in the late afternoon sky and is blasting in from behind Vern and his horse. When they hit the river, the water explodes around them and the sun makes it all dance in slow motion. What an amazing picture of freedom and adventure.

I immediately slam on the brakes and, as Vern comes sliding up beside me, I say, "I just saw your life." Laughing and out of breath, he asks me what I mean. I describe what I have just witnessed: a friend living life to the fullest. Even at eighty-two, Vern had just created one of my life's unique peak experiences. I expect that part of the ride may have been a peak experience for Vern, as well. I'll never forget that moment, that picture of Vern. It embodied everything about him—guts, freedom, and adventure.

Is there a picture of you that captures everything about you?

I didn't realize it then but we had been experiencing what Dana and I now call "Free Reining." The symbolism of watching Vern crossing the Sheep River stayed with me. Some time later, I made the connection between Vern's freedom and spirit to the notion that, subconsciously, we all have placed a bit in our mouth. Without realizing it, at times, we hold ourselves back, staying in the Comfort Zone and possibly missing out on some of life's unique and wonderful peak experiences.

In a calculated and deliberate way, Vern and I had decided to take the pressure off the bit in our horses' mouths. In the same way, we were metaphorically taking the pressure off the imaginary bits we all have in our minds.

Free Reining was born from the experience Hal and Vern had when they decided to let their horses go, to run as fast as they could down that twisting mountain trail, charging through the river time and time again. To some, this would appear to be foolish and downright dangerous. To Vern and Hal, who knew the terrain and what to expect from their horses, it was just pure fun, excitement, and adventure. Sure, it was out of their Comfort Zones, but not as far out as for someone less familiar with riding horses in such a situation. For some people, letting the horses blaze would be insane. But for Hal and Vern, letting the horses merely walk down the trail seemed mundane.

Vern and Hal had "been there, done that" so many times before. They intentionally let the reins go in order to create a peak experience. Sure, there was a risk that it could have ended badly—a wreck, an injury, or worse—but so could driving your car on a city freeway or getting too close to a soft shoulder on a beautiful country road. But in these driving examples, most of us don't have an overriding fear holding us back. Why is that? Why are we not metaphorically pulling back on the reins when we get behind the wheel?

We believe it is because of familiarity. We have been there, done that many times before. For most of us, driving a car is well within our Comfort Zone. But that has not always been the case, has it? Can you remember the first time you drove a car? Maybe it was on a country road, so that you wouldn't kill someone the first time out! Maybe it was with your dad, taking you out for the first time and telling you not to get too close to the ditch. You would over-correct with the steering or maybe hit the brakes, sending everyone in the car lurching forward. Not so comfortable back then, was it? Fun, but really nervous. Now, there is nothing to it, but back then, many of us metaphorically had the reins pulled in tight: sitting up straight, our backs not against the seat, our hands sweating as we held that death grip at "10 and 2" on the steering wheel, right leg quivering like a rattlesnake ready to strike that brake pedal at any time. All it took was a "Careful" from dad and everyone in the car would go lurching forward again, snapping their necks, with howling laughter to be heard a mile away.

We can probably all remember our first time behind the wheel. It was a peak experience in our life and came with a sense of freedom, empowerment, and entry into young adulthood. For months, we would be cautious with our driving, not wanting to have an accident or get a ticket. The more we drove and ventured out of our Comfort Zone, the more comfortable we became. The longer we practiced and pushed our level of comfort, the more our Comfort Zone was expanded to include everyday driving. We don't think twice now about getting into the driver's seat.

But let's take this driving comfort idea a step further. Have you ever wondered what it would be like to drive a Formula One race car or perhaps race cross-country in the desert or in the mountains? In both instances at incredible speeds, with a high risk of injury or even possible death? What goes through your mind as you think about trying that? Probably, "Not a chance. That's nuts. That's insane." Maybe for us, but not for those who actually race. But you and I put the brakes on in our minds. We pull back on the reins: "I couldn't do that. No way."

You might be thinking right now that this book is crazy. "Are they telling me I should try driving a race car?" Well, maybe. That's up to you. We're just trying to stretch your boundaries of comfort. Let's keep going. Let us ask you another question. Would you ride shotgun (passenger seat) with a professional race-car driver just to experience the thrill of going that fast? Just twice around the track at 200 miles an hour? We bet many of you would, and the reason why we think that would be a safe bet is that most of you wouldn't think twice about doing things like zip-lining, ripping around a roller coaster track, or jumping on a double Ferris wheel. Most of us will do that just for the thrill, to push ourselves out of our Comfort Zone and to intentionally create a mini peak experience. We'll push the boundaries if we feel some degree of safety. What we mean by that is that when we take a ride in that race car or jump onto the roller coaster or Ferris wheel, we are still under someone else's control or in a safe, reasonably predictable environment. Certainly we have let the inhibiting reins of fear relax a bit by even participating, but we are not in control.

For a moment, can you think about putting yourself in a potential peak-experience situation where you are in total control? The experience you are trying to create is totally up to you. You are not a bystander (or by-sitter), where the race-car driver is in control or where the amusement park ride operator is in control.

By pulling back on our own reins, we may subconsciously be saying, "I can't. There's no way. I'm not good enough. Who would find me interesting? I'm too old." Everyone at different times puts on the brakes. Fear is the great crippler; lack of confidence is the great inhibitor.

To physically experience what we are sometimes mentally doing to ourselves, let's try a little Free Reining right now. Humour us; play along. Take your right index finger and hook it in the right corner of your mouth. Do the same with your left. Now pull backward with your fingers drawing back the corners of your mouth. Come on now. Put the book down for five seconds and try it. It will be your first step toward truly understanding how Free Reining can change your life. Try it. No one is watching.

If you actually tried it, you will now have a sense of how a horse sometimes feels with an inexperienced rider constantly pulling back on the reins, generally out of fear or lack of ability. You may also have an idea of what a person feels like who has a bit in their own mouth, with the reins regularly being pulled back. It's those fears and perceived lack of abilities (self-confidence) that mentally keep pulling back on the corners of our mouths, holding us back.

There are two key components of Free Reining: letting go of the reins and dreaming of possibilities. These components are intertwined. Let us show you how. Remember John Davidson's advice: "You can start by dreaming. The beautiful thing about dreaming is that the sky's the limit and you can dream as big as you want, financially or otherwise." Dreaming involves creativity and inspiration. It involves reflection and the freedom to think of possibilities. And here is where letting go comes in. It is extremely difficult to think freely and creatively when we are being held back by pressures, fears, trepidation, potential risks, anxieties, or just the daily grind and busyness (the bits in our mouth). Possibility-thinking focuses us into the future, but all of the bits in our mouth keep us anchored in the present or in the past. Did you catch the word "anchored?" They hold us back and limit our creativity. To effectively Free Rein, we have to take control of our reins and release the pressure on whichever bits may be holding us back.

We need to take time to mentally shake off the constraints of our everyday lives and look for glimpses into the Lifeworth Zone. Just like the horse shaking its head up and down trying to create some slack in the reins, we need to release the pressure from our various bits or constraints in order to think about the type of peak experience we would like to create. The constant pulling back of different bits tends to override our ability to be creative. We need to identify and address each of these bits, fears, or anxieties. Write them down. Address each one by trying to "let go" of the reins. Ask yourself one simple question: "What's the worst that can happen if I take the pressure off this particular bit?" Go through them one by one. By creating slack in the reins and by relaxing the pressure, we open ourselves to thinking creatively about how to break out of our Comfort Zone and create a peak experience in the Lifeworth Zone.

Once the pressure is off, continue to Free Rein by dreaming of possibilities. Think about peak experiences you had in the past. Try to feel the intensity of the emotions you were experiencing at the time. Can you build on these past peak experiences? Think about the peak experiences of the people interviewed for this book. Do other ideas come to mind that could be adapted to fit your current life and resources, your marble bag? Review your answers to the questions we asked at the end of the previous chapters. What possibilities come to mind? ■

SO NOW WHAT?

We have introduced you to the concept of Free Reining, which involves loosening the reins, taking the pressure off the bits in your mind that might be holding you back, and dreaming about potential peak experiences. Peak experiences happen throughout our lives whether we plan them or not. Sometimes they just happen, occurring out of the blue. Other times, peak experiences have been well-planned-out adventures. Having this knowledge now allows each of us to take the pressure off the psychological bits in our mind and to make an intentional attempt at Free Reining, to create that exciting, exhilarating, and wonderful peak experience in life. How do we do that? Here are three key questions to help you dream.

1. "When was the *last* time you did something for the *first* time?" Great question! Even as the authors of *Lifeworth*, when we asked ourselves this question, we both found that there had been many stretches in our lives when we had not done something new for quite some time. So we took our own advice and rectified that. Hal and his wife, Penny, planned a trip to climb Mount Kilimanjaro. Dana decided to start rock climbing with one of his sons, Jeff. It had been too long since breaking out of our own Comfort Zones. So when was the *last* time you did something for the *first* time? How long ago was it? Can you remember the emotions you experienced? Does remembering that experience invoke an internal drive or desire to create another new peak experience in your life?

2. You may have to think about this second question for a little bit. "What are you afraid of?" We are all afraid of something. What are your fears? Writing down your fears helps you to see them more clearly.

3. The last question we asked ourselves is a bit of a tongue twister: "What did you used to do that you liked to do and would like to do again?" You might have to read it again. Is there something you may have done years ago but for various reasons, maybe just the busyness of life, you stopped doing? Something that gave you a deep sense of joy and accomplishment? Something you would like to start doing again?

Remember, beyond fear is freedom!

CHAPTER EIGHT

CODY'S DREAM

—LINDSAY SEARS

The highest reward for a person's toil is not what
they get for it, but what they become by it.

JOHN RUSKIN

L indsay Sears is a world-class barrel racer in the Professional Rodeo
Association and the Women's Professional Rodeo Association. At
twenty-nine years old, she has had a life full of peak experiences of the
type most people wouldn't have in an entire lifetime. She hails from a
ranch set in the foothills of the Alberta Rockies, growing up near the small ranching town of Nanton, south of Calgary.

Lindsay has been around horses all her life, and attended Texas Tech University
on a rodeo scholarship. Following graduation, she tried to figure out what she
wanted to do with her life. She gave an office job a chance, but soon realized that
the business world was not for her. Although she did not win many barrel races
during her high school years, the competitions sparked something inside this remarkable young woman, something that would shape the next phase of her life.
Lindsay currently lives in Texas. Here is her story in her own words.

• • • •

What has happened in my life in the last five years is hard to describe, because it changed me so much. I lived on a ranch, and my parents didn't want me to be a barrel racer at all. Barrel racing is a highly competitive timed event where we cross a starting line at full speed and race around three barrels set up in a large triangle in a cloverleaf pattern in the arena, and sprint back to the finish line where we started. The separation between the top riders can be in the hundredths of a second. It's a wildly popular event for the rodeo fans.

Growing up, we had the local Nanton Nite rodeo, and I always wanted to go because my best friend in elementary school was a barrel racer. Her parents had really nice horses for her to ride, and my parents wouldn't spend the money on a barrel horse, so I would just ride a feedlot horse or a ranch horse. I would get my butt kicked every weekend.

And, to be honest, I was not good at barrel racing. It is an event that is about 90 percent horse and 10 percent rider. You are only as good as your horse, but you also have to be able to ride it and manage it. My barrel-racing career early on was a hobby, something I did for fun. My dad, Rick Sears, wanted me to do other things in life: go to school, get a degree, get a job. But he always said, "Do something you love, something you're passionate about." He always told me that in order to be successful, you have to be passionate about what you're doing.

I barrel raced for fun, but when I came home from university to work for my family's business, I realized that I wasn't so passionate about the business. I was dissatisfied with what I was doing. I asked myself what I wanted to do in life. And I thought, "Well, I really think I want to barrel race." I told Dad, and he said, "If that's what you want to do, I'll help you do it. I'll loan you the money to buy the horse. Go find a horse and we'll see what happens."

I don't know if my dad had been willing to do that all along, but I first had to go through the steps of going to university, getting good grades, and graduating with a degree. I went to Texas Tech University and received a Bachelor of Science degree in Agricultural and Applied Economics. After all, barrel racing is just a sport. It doesn't last forever. Once I was done, what was I going to do? That was always my dad's worry. I had to have a back-up plan. I had to be able to go out, get a job, and be able to make a living. So it was not that my family did not support my barrel racing, but it was definitely not something that was a focus right from the start. But Dad told me, "Okay, I will support you 100 percent, but I expect *200* percent from you. Barrel racing needs to be what you eat, breathe, and think about. Be passionate."

And so that's how it all started. Once the decision was made, it just seemed to flow from there. Everything kind of fell into place, I think, because I made the decision to commit completely and totally to racing.

We realized that we needed more horsepower. We needed a faster horse, a different calibre of horse than we have ever had. While I was attending university in Texas I called a friend and told her what I wanted to do. I asked her if she knew of any horses for sale that fit that description. She said she didn't know of any right then, but she had this five-year-old mare that she really thought was talented. I said, "I don't know. Five years old? I want to rodeo. Where has this horse been?" The answer was almost nowhere, so I took a pass on that horse. I was looking for something a little older, a little more seasoned. That was around August 2005.

A couple of months went by and my friend called me back and said, "I really think that you'll like this horse, the one I told you about. Martha is her name and she will be at my place. Come by and see her." So in January 2006, my mom, Susan, and I went to Texas and I rode the horse.

Martha was just five years old, but I knew instantly that I really liked her. It was the weirdest thing. It was one of those times where a person has a gut feeling. But the horse didn't fit the description of what I wanted; it was probably too early in her life. Martha didn't have any barrel-racing history or any experience. She was green, as we call it in the horse world. I called my dad and told him that, although on paper Martha didn't fit the description of what I was looking for, I had a gut feeling about the horse. He told me that in business and in life you have to take chances.

For all kinds of reasons, I shouldn't have bought that horse, but I did anyway. We paid more than Martha was worth considering what she had done up to that point in time. It was a significant amount, but I just knew that I needed this horse. That was January and, later that year, in December, I qualified for my first National Finals Rodeo [NFR] in Las Vegas on Martha.

But it wasn't just a normal start with Martha. It was weird. I bought her, and three days later in Los Fresnos, Texas, her first rodeo, she fell down and bruised her gaskin bone. It was a very serious injury and it happened so fast. Martha got sores the size of a volleyball high up on the inside of her back leg. We drained them for two months. I couldn't ride her at all. It was difficult. Martha's leg was very stiff for three or four weeks.

Although she was very talented, I found that Martha was hard to look after. It took a long time to figure out all her little quirks, and what she needed to be happy. I discovered quickly that you can't change her environment a whole lot, or she won't eat or drink on the road.

Martha had all sorts of things that made it difficult to rodeo on her, because, when we rodeo, we're gone three hundred days a year. If the horse doesn't eat or drink on the road, it causes a huge problem. I thought, "Oh my God, I've spent all this money on this horse and she doesn't eat or drink. What did I get myself into? My dad's going to kill me."

The first month I had her, I was crappin' bricks. I couldn't even put her in a horse stall. The first week I took Martha away from her home, I put her in a stall in Fort Worth, Texas. The stall had a dirt floor, and when

I went out to check on her about an hour later, she had dug a hole. She was just lathered in sweat. I thought, "This horse is nuts. I bought this horse without first taking her to a race. What the heck am I going to do with this thing?"

It was a bit of a panic at first. I knew this wasn't going to be easy. And it wasn't. The first year was definitely hard. When I brought her home to Canada, Martha still wasn't doing well. She didn't eat or drink consistently. Then an idea came to me. I had this old horse named Quick, which I had rodeo'd on during high school. Quick was a mare and had had two babies. She was a really calm, motherly type of horse, so I put her beside Martha. Instantly, they connected. Now Martha eats and drinks normally and stays calm in her stall. These days, the only time Martha is without Quick is when Martha is in the arena. The two horses have to go everywhere together.

Martha is a very talented horse, in the sense that she is very confident when she is running the barrels in the arena, but she's very insecure with everything else. Quick knickers at her when Martha is upset. She scratches her neck when Martha is nervous. It's the oddest thing you have ever seen. They talk about how all the great horses in history had a buddy of some type: a goat, a pony, another horse. I don't know why, but it seems like a lot of the great racehorses also had a buddy. Martha now has a buddy. Quick is loyal to Martha, and they get along great.

By April 2006, Martha was healthy, so we went to California. I ended up winning the Auburn and Red Bluff, California, rodeos. Although Martha was still green, she started winning. Part of the reason, I think, was that when Martha was hurt, I spent lots of hours with her. It gave me a lot of time to just bond with my horse. I think the early injury was the best thing that ever happened, because I had to be with her more than usual. I was treating her three or four times a day, not including the twice-a-day feedings. I spent five or six hours a day with Martha, doctoring her and caring for her. We became an inseparable team.

I don't know how many rodeos I've won on Martha, but the actual titles include 2008 World Champion, 2009 Reserve World Champion, and 2010 Reserve World Champion. I have won rodeos in San Antonio, Houston, Tucson, Calgary, Omaha, Reno, Dallas, Cheyenne, and countless other places. While riding Martha, I was the first ladies barrel racer to ever earn over $300,000 in a regular rodeo season. I have the earnings record for regular season earnings, and I have the record for the most amount of money won in a single event at the National Finals Rodeo. In 2008, I won $450,000 on Martha; 2008 was definitely the year. I think I won first at every major rodeo. San Antonio, Houston, Calgary, Cheyenne, Omaha, and Dallas rodeos were all firsts. It was one of those years when everything fell into place.

I paid $60,000 for Martha, and my total earnings are well over $1 million. I could probably sell her for a lot of money, but I'll never sell Martha. We're part of each other now. And at the end of 2008, when everything just seemed to be going right, my dad said, "Be prepared; it's not going to happen like this all the time. Remember how you got here. Remember what it took to get you to this point in your life. This year is a very, very lucky year."

Dad was right. The year 2009 didn't start off well. I struggled the entire year with one thing after another. Nothing seemed to go right. Don't get me wrong; I was still winning. On paper, I had a good year, but everything else in my life was falling apart, from my horse getting hurt, to breaking my leg, to being sick all year and not knowing why. Then we found out in October that I had a large cyst on my ovaries that would require major surgery right away.

It was one of those years that make a person take a look at their life. I was definitely thinking, "Okay, I have achieved what I wanted to achieve in this business." But I wasn't having fun anymore. Racing wasn't something that I looked forward to. Martha injured herself at the Bremerton, Washington, rodeo when she was trying to stop after her run. She slipped, slammed into the fence, and hurt her front legs and feet on the fence. Maybe this was a sign that I needed to do something else with my life. Maybe I needed to step away and look for a different job. When I was growing up, I had thought I would probably work in the corporate world, so I was considering that. I was really thinking about quitting the rodeo life.

Then, out of the blue, I received a phone call from a friend of Cody Stephens. Cody was a bull rider and, by the age of twenty-three, had made the American Cowboys Rodeo Association bull riding finals five years in a row. My friend explained that Cody was battling leukemia and was about to undergo a bone marrow transplant. However, one of his life goals was to meet me and, to do that, he wanted to go to the WPRA finals in Tulsa, Oklahoma, where I would be. But because of his condition, Cody could not leave the hospital, and my friend asked if I could call him. I asked why he wanted to meet me. Why me? I was just a barrel racer from Alberta. She said Cody just really wanted to meet Lindsay Sears, that he admired me and had a crush on me. I was surprised because he was a young bull rider. He wasn't a barrel racer. I found it was the oddest thing, but thought, "Sure, why not? I'll call him."

It was quite a strange call. A bit awkward in the beginning, but I think, even after a few minutes, Cody sensed that something wasn't quite right, that the spark wasn't in me. I hadn't mentioned anything specific to him, but I think he could tell that I was considering quitting. He wanted to talk about rodeo and about the NFR in Las Vegas, two weeks away. Cody asked if I was excited about the NFR, and I said that I was getting ready. I think he knew that I wasn't very excited about it.

It seemed that during the whole conversation he was trying to motivate me for the NFR. And I thought to myself, here he was having a bone marrow transplant the next day and he is more concerned about motivating me. In reality, the NFR was nothing compared to what he was about to go through. It was as if it never crossed his mind that he was having a bone marrow transplant.

I remember thinking to myself during the whole conversation, "Oh my gosh, here I've been feeling sorry for myself, thinking I need to do something else with my life. And he would have given his right arm to be at the NFR." That's what he was dreaming about. That's what he was lying there thinking about at night. That's what kept him alive, in a sense. It made me realize how lucky I really was and how good I had it. Here's a person in a lot worse situation, with a lot more serious things going on in his life, and he's not at all concerned about himself. He was more concerned about other people around him.

After about thirty minutes, I hung up the phone. I remember looking at my mom and saying, "I'm going to go to Vegas and I'm going to win a buckle for Cody." It had always been a ritual of mine at the NFR to give a "go around" buckle that I won to the people who helped me get there. I'd keep one from each year for me, usually the first one, but then I would give the rest to people who had been supportive.

There are ten nights in the National Finals Rodeo event each December, and each night is like a rodeo in itself. We barrel race each of the ten nights and you have an opportunity to win ten go around buckles. Of course, each night they pay out winnings and, at the end of the NFR, the world champion is the person with the most winnings, including not only a person's NFR earnings but regular season earnings, as well. I was going into the NFR in second place. Of course, everyone thought my main goal would be to win a world title, but I felt more motivated to just win a go around buckle for Cody. That was more important to me.

I knew that Cody was never going to have the opportunity to go there. If I could do anything for him, I could bring the NFR to him. I knew that it was his lifelong goal and dream to be in the NFR himself.

I thought if that's the one thing I can do for this person, that's what I need to do. I wanted to bring Cody a buckle. It was the start of realizing what is important in life.

But at this point, my horse didn't even have horseshoes on. We weren't sure if Martha was going to be able to run at the NFR. This was ten days before the NFR started in December, and I hadn't ridden her since September. Martha was just coming off a three-month rest due to an injury, so winning the title was a long shot. It was not going to be easy. But we scrambled to get ready and, after the second go around, I had won a buckle for Cody. I was relieved. Now I could focus on trying to win the world title, because winning that buckle for Cody was the most important thing for me to do that year at the NFR.

I ended up not winning the world championship. I came second in the world (Reserve Champion). I should have been disappointed, but I wasn't. I knew that I had tried my best and, under the circumstances, I had done well. Being in the situation I was in, with Martha injured, me not being healthy, and knowing that I had to have major surgery immediately after the NFR, I was happy with the result. I was somewhat disappointed, of course, because, as a competitor, you want to win, to be the champion. But as important as it seemed, it really wasn't important after all. I kept telling myself over and over again, "There will be another rodeo, and there is more to life. The gold buckle is important, but, in the scheme of life, winning all the time isn't everything."

As for the buckles, to me they are just buckles, another marble in the bag. If they just sat on a shelf in my house, I wouldn't even look at them. I wouldn't even fully appreciate them. If I can give one to somebody who would appreciate it, and in Cody's case bring a lifelong dream to reality, that means more to me than keeping the buckle on a shelf. I know what I've accomplished. I don't have to look at something to remind me. It might mean a lot more to someone else who has helped me get there. It feels so good to give some of it away.

That year, after the 2009 NFR finals, I had surgery on December 21. A cyst on the top of my ovaries was causing a lot of problems. It was a fairly large tumour, and it needed to be dealt with. After the surgery, I planned to fly to see Cody on the weekend of January 20 to give him his buckle. But I received a phone call the morning of January 13 from a friend of Cody's saying that his mom wanted me to come right away, because they didn't think Cody was going to make it through the next twenty-four hours. This was about 11 A.M., so I packed a bag and raced to the airport. I got to Kansas City that night about 7:30. Cody's family picked me up at the airport, and we drove straight to the hospital.

During the whole time I was on the plane, I was trying to think of what I was going to say when I walked into that hospital room. I thought about it a lot, but when it came down to that moment I still didn't know. What do you say to this individual who is about to lose a battle that he has fought so hard to win, so courageously? He motivated me for the NFR. How am I going to comfort him?

I think all of us have idolized someone in our lives. When you finally get the opportunity to meet them, you sometimes think, "Oh my gosh, this is not what I expected them to be." I remember saying to my friend, "I just don't want to be a disappointment to him." I was so afraid that I wouldn't be who he thought I was. I didn't want him to have anything but positive and encouraging feelings at that stage of the game. He needed everything to be perfect. I hoped I was what he pictured me to be.

I had never been more nervous in my entire life. My heart rate was definitely off the charts the entire time. While I was walking down the hallway to his hospital room, I remember thinking that, of all the experiences in my life, there had only been one other time when I was so nervous. It was at the 2009 NFR when it had come down to one run for the world championship. It came down to the tenth round and I lost out by 0.05 seconds—a bit of a heartbreaker. I was nervous for that, but you couldn't even compare these two experiences. Sure, I was nervous getting ready for world championships and world titles, but walking in to meet Cody face-to-face was incredibly nerve-racking. My heart was pounding. In barrel racing, the only person affected by the outcome of a race is me. In this case, I was about to possibly influence Cody's life and give him some final peace and happiness at a point when time was running out.

I walked into that room and, of course, seeing him was a shock, because he was so sick. He was a bright yellow colour. I had never been on a cancer floor in a hospital before or even seen anyone who has had chemotherapy. Nor had I been so up-front-and-personal, so close to someone who was fighting for his very next breath. It definitely was shocking. A person quickly realizes how lucky they are. I had just had a tumour removed, but, at the time I was visiting Cody, I didn't have the results of my tests back yet. I was worried about having cancer and also wondering about my ability to ever have children. There were a lot of life-changing decisions going on in my world at the time I visited Cody. Meeting him made all of my problems seem non-existent, because, on my worst day, I was lucky in comparison to his situation. It was after my visit to Cody that I found out my tumour was benign. Not only was I having feelings about my own future, I was having feelings of empathy for him. While I was trying to deal with my own situation, I was meeting Cody to present him with the buckle, trying to put a smile on his face and make the last few hours of his life as good as I could. That was my goal for this meeting.

And when I walked in, Cody smiled. His mom, to this day, says he hadn't smiled in a long time. The thing you have to know about Cody is that it hurt him to touch his hand. He was in so much pain. He hadn't been embraced in who knows how many weeks. His mouth was full of sores. He couldn't swallow. It was just unbelievable. At that point, the doctors and nurses were just trying to do everything they could to make him comfortable, and there wasn't much they could do. Cody wasn't eating. They were just giving him enough fluids to sustain him.

The first thing I said was, "Hi Cody. I'm Lindsay." He couldn't see very well; the medication blurred his vision. You had to get fairly close for him to make out who you were.

He said, "I don't know what to say."

I said, "You don't have to say anything at all. I'm just happy to be here."

That was how the conversation started off. I never felt more satisfied in my entire life. I was sitting in the hospital room with him, just visiting. All my nervousness quickly melted away. It made the world titles seem absolutely irrelevant. I had worked very hard for those titles. That was all I'd basically done for the last five years of my life. I had given up a lot of things in my life to try and win that world title, but it seemed so unimportant now.

Hal and Dana asked me what I thought my definition of *Lifeworth* is at only twenty-nine years old. What does a life worth living look like to me? I was raised to always have a goal, to work hard, to do the best I can, to be kind to others, and to try to be successful at what I do. And, while those are still my beliefs, my views have changed with respect to having "things." Before meeting Cody, I actually thought that material things were important, that it was important to have a nice car, have nice clothes, and all that. After I walked out of the hospital room having met Cody, all that was much less meaningful to me.

Six months ago, what I thought was important in my life means nothing to me now. I know you need money and I know you need these "things" to survive, but money does not make my life worth living. More money might bring me more comfort, but the material things don't create a life worth living.

The experience of meeting Cody has shaped the way I think about my life. I realize now my purpose in life is to think of others more, in a positive and generous way. If each one of us can perform one act of kindness that will change another person's life in a positive way, then that is a life worth living. Now knowing that I can be an example for the younger generation, I feel more aware of how I can enrich others. I didn't realize that some people might actually look up to me, that I might be someone that a little girl might admire someday. I didn't realize that until I met Cody. In his final hours, Cody helped me to know what is important in life. What Cody found important was his family and treating others well. Every nurse in that hospital loved Cody. Never once did he get upset. It hurt to take his blood pressure. It hurt for him to roll over. He was in an unbelievable amount of pain, but never once did he take it out on anyone else.

I hope to be remembered as someone who cared about others, someone who put others' needs in front of her own. I hope that I will have made a difference in someone's life in a positive way. The experience of meeting Cody completely changed my idea about who I want to be and how I want to treat other people. I want to treat people like Cody treated people. He never put himself in front of others. I hope to be remembered as I remember Cody. I don't know if that will ever be possible, but I'm sure going to work at it. Even after making so much money at such a young age, I now realize that it doesn't matter how much money you have. If you don't have your health and your family, you have nothing.

I think that so many people get caught up in what they think is important in life until they have a peak experience, such as I have had with meeting Cody. A lot of people think material things are the answer and having a lot of money is what determines self-worth, but I don't think that is what enriches a person's life. What enriches your life is an experience, such as I had with meeting Cody. It was the best thing I have ever done in my life. It's the happiest I've ever felt, and it's the saddest I've ever felt. It's the most satisfied I've ever been, and it's the hardest thing I've done in my life. I walked away from that hospital room with so many emotions that I didn't even know what to feel. I was a wreck for a week after. I just couldn't sort out my feelings. It changed my entire perspective on life. I still find myself thinking about it for hours on end.

At the end of the day, if money isn't that important, if growing your business isn't that important, if winning the world title really isn't that important, what is? The answer to that question, I think, is that it's anything you want in your life that will also positively change someone else's life. That's a life worth living.

Cody passed away the next day, January 17, 2010. His bright smile faded away into the night, and the world lost a truly unique human being. I was going to see Cody to help him, but it turns out he helped me. If Cody got anything out of our meeting, I'll never know. But he gave me a gift that I will carry with me for the rest of my life. Cody changed my life for the better. I don't think you can put a price tag on that. ■

SO NOW WHAT?

Lindsay's story provides us with a great example of taking a risk to achieve a peak experience when she decided on gut instinct to buy her horse, Martha. The two have been a winning combination. Lindsay's story also gives us examples of different types of peak experiences. Each time she wins a major rodeo or the world or reserved champion titles is a peak experience for her because the competition is fierce at the professional level. Setting records for earnings won have been peak experiences. She faced a different type of peak experience in her battles with an operation that could have had a significant impact on her career. And, finally, she laid out the emotions of her peak experiences of meeting Cody, winning the buckle for him, and of the significant impact he had on her life.

- Has there been a time in your life when your attempts to support or comfort someone else also had a profound effect on you?

- What feelings did you experience? What impact did it have on the other person? On you?

- Are there opportunities in your future to create similar peak experiences of making a difference for someone truly in need?

- What marbles would you have to use from your bag? Your Time Marbles? Talent Marbles? Treasure Marbles? Which type of marbles do you think would have the most meaning for you and create a peak experience with a significant impact?

CHAPTER NINE

GETTING OFF THE COUCH

— JEANELLE MITCHELL, SUSAN WETMORE, DAWN STRAKA

If you want others to be happy, practice compassion.
If you want to be happy, practice compassion.

THE DALAI LAMA

The people whose stories we have told thus far have achieved significant milestones and reached their personal peak experiences in
unique and sometimes dramatic ways. But peak experiences occur
in everyone's lives and can be of different magnitudes. What is most
important is that the peak experience actually takes you out of your Comfort Zone.

In this chapter we share the stories of three individuals who achieved peak
experiences without making huge transitions in their day-to-day lives. They pushed
into the Lifeworth Zone right from where they were in life. These women, from
various parts of Canada, have clearly identified their life's passion and purpose and
have found unique ways to fulfill their goal of making a positive impact in the lives
of others. Each time they reached out to help others, they created a peak experience
within their Lifeworth Zone. They moved out of their Comfort Zone and aligned
with their core talents and passion.

• • • •

J eanelle Mitchell of Toronto, Ontario, was motivated by compassion and a deep desire to help her family when they were in need. She decided to rocket herself out of her Comfort Zone and write two cookbooks, which became Canadian best-sellers. Here's how she got there.

"My sister, who lives in the Maritimes, has experienced a decade of agony and heartache. Ten years ago, just after his high school graduation, her son was the unfortunate victim of a serious car accident, broadsided by a transport truck, leaving him brain-damaged and in a coma for nine months. It has taken the last eight years for his family to settle the claim and receive a structured settlement. Today, my nephew is making the best of his situation as a paraplegic. Unfortunately, the family tragedy and heartache didn't stop there.

"My sister's husband is currently battling cancer and her third son is suffering from life-threatening emphysema. With the household income decimated due to accidents and illness, the medical and legal bills quickly mounted to the point where bankruptcy was the only option. My sister's tough luck and heartache eventually became too much for me. I could not sit idly by and watch her family suffer. I wanted to help financially in whatever way I could. I have a passion for food and cooking and decided I would write a soup cookbook.

"It took me two years to write *For the Love of Soup* and have it printed by a friend. I didn't know much about self-publishing, so I organized an initial book launch on my own in the spring of 2000. I invited family and friends to a local cricket club and sold eight hundred books in just two hours! I was absolutely amazed that I sold that many at the launch. I was also amazed by the book's continued success. Mostly through word of mouth, sales shot to four thousand in no time.

"The sales increased so quickly that I didn't think I could continue to do the whole job out of my home. I decided I needed to hire a professional publisher. Eventually I contracted with a Vancouver publisher who upgraded the graphics and physical look of the book. We officially launched it across Canada in September 2000. To date, *For the Love of Soup* has sold about twenty-five thousand copies. It felt so great to have the book become a success, and it was very rewarding to be able to help my sister and her family. I was encouraged to write a second book, which was also a challenge, taking two years to write. We launched *For the Love of Salad* in the spring of 2010 and it has now sold close to ten thousand copies."

We asked Jeanelle what impact these peak experiences have had on her life. "After retiring from the airlines, I undertook the project of writing *For the Love of Soup*. My plan was to self-publish, which I did, and had five thousand copies printed. That was a big investment but I felt confident that I would sell them. After selling all the books within three months, I then called a publisher and told them my story. They took on the project. That was the most exciting thing that ever happened to me! A dream come true! The proceeds have been tremendously helpful to my sister and her family."

Jeanelle, a recent retiree, was truly in a Comfort Zone, although her sister's family's suffering weighed heavily on her mind. It was her passion to help her sister and her family that pulled her out of her Comfort Zone into the Lifeworth Zone to write that first book. She had to let go of the fear of writing a book that might not sell or might not be "good enough." Her peak experience was driven by the emotion of a strong family connection and her desire to help her family in any way she could. It couldn't help but pull her into her future.

The second woman in our trio is Susan Wetmore, who moved from London, Ontario, to a coast-side home on Salt Spring Island, British Columbia, in 2009. Terry Zavitz of London, Ontario, introduced us to Susan. Susan intrigued us with stories of her volunteer efforts with the Canadian Executive Services Organization (CESO) over the past eight years. CESO is a volunteer-based organization that plays an active role in improving social and economic conditions that hinder progress in Canada and around the world.

Susan has volunteered for different CESO assignments, internationally and nationally. "Countries that we have worked in are ones that Canada has had an agreement with," she said. "I have been fortunate to be able to volunteer in countries such as Ukraine, Grenada, Burkina Faso, Philippines, Armenia, Honduras, Tajikistan, Haiti, Cameroon, and my own country, Canada. I have seen a lot of the world, but it hasn't exactly been places high on the tourist list. I volunteer to help small hotels and restaurants improve and grow their business and contribute to the strength of their local economy. I absolutely love what I do. I have a huge passion for helping others grow and achieve new goals."

When Susan works with a host restaurant or hotel, she looks at it from many different perspectives and from all aspects of the business. "I have the opportunity to meet and spend time with both the owners and the staff of each business. I get involved in every aspect from the front to the back," she said. "I look at menus, kitchen designs, customer service, and training, as well as issues concerning the environment. Most important, I gather input from everyone on how they could improve and grow their business.

"In some of these countries I experienced a huge cultural shift. When I travelled to Tajikistan, next door to Afghanistan, it was during Ramadan, a Muslim holiday. I wasn't sure what to wear. I wasn't sure how open they would be to a white, grey-haired, Christian woman. But everything worked out fine, and I got along very well."

When we asked Susan why she would take these volunteer assignments to underdeveloped and sometimes dangerous countries, she told us there were a couple of reasons. "First, I grew up in a family where my mother and father believed that our job in life was to give back to the community," she said. "Second, I have found over the years that just being there, listening to what people have to say, advocating on behalf of the staff, and meeting with the owners is a huge help. Every day I am there,

I have an opportunity to put my teaching and communication skills to valuable use. I don't tell them what to do. I just offer my observations on how they can improve their businesses. Women, in particular, have a hard time creating opportunities to move into management positions. Unfortunately, that's a big problem and it's also one that drives me."

Susan sees generosity and enduring spirit in the countries she visits. "When I come home, I go into a bit of culture shock," she said. "I think, in Canada, many people have lost their perspective as to what is important in life. Going to these underdeveloped countries certainly grounds me. It helps me decide what is important and also how to appreciate other cultures, both overseas and in Canada."

We asked Susan what her personal definition of *Lifeworth* would be. Without hesitation, she said, "A life worth living for me is to be able to give to others, to share my interests and skills, to grow with them and to learn from them. I don't think there is any greater gift than that. I have had many assignments that have been amazing experiences. The relationships I have developed with many of these people during my different assignments are unbelievable.

"I think that my purpose in life is to continue to mentor, to continue to share my skill sets, whether it's with hotels, restaurants, or individuals."

Susan is a great example of someone who is using her Talent Marbles to follow her life's purpose and to help others follow theirs. By her own admission, she is an individual who likes to keep reinventing herself, taking different courses and programs, and being involved with different organizations to expand her skill sets. When she is mentoring others, she encourages them to discover what they are truly interested in and to try to identify their core skill sets. Most important, when back in Canada, Susan encourages people to just get involved.

"It doesn't matter what you do, just get off the couch," she said. "I don't care if you go help out at the food bank or the literacy centre, just get out."

As with most of us, Susan has her own Comfort Zone, which sometimes becomes too comfortable. She is driven to break out of it by using her Talent Marbles to help those struggling to meet their core needs and create some semblance of a Comfort Zone in their own country. The sacrifice for Susan did not come through using her Treasure Marbles; she told us that her travel and living expenses were covered by CESO. Instead, it comes from using up a significant number of her Time Marbles and volunteering those Talent Marbles that she feels are aligned with her life purpose, regardless of the economic or political situation she may have been venturing into. The desire to help others grow and become more self-sufficient has been part of her life since she was a child; it was and continues to be second nature. Much like Jeanelle Mitchell, Susan's passion couldn't help but pull her into her future and to different peak experiences around the world.

Finally, we would like to introduce Dawn Straka, who lives in Peterborough, Ontario. Heather Stelzer and Terry Windrem introduced us to Dawn.

Early in her adult life, Dawn had a few unplanned emotionally charged peak experiences. Her father passed away when she was only nineteen and part way through her nursing studies. Years later, in 1986, at the age of forty-seven, she lost her husband to cancer and became a single parent, having to raise two young boys ages seven and eleven.

"That definitely was a tough experience while we were living in Toronto," Dawn said. "I remember coming to the realization that my husband was dying, and my mother had just died a few months before. I was an orphan, and now I was going to be a widow. It was a very emotional experience. As bad as it was, it certainly spurred me on to try to recognize how responsible I was for these two kids and having to take on all of the duties of not only raising them, but providing for all of us. The kids were doing fine, but I needed to move to a smaller community. Peterborough [a small city northeast of Toronto] was wonderful that way."

Dawn provides a great example of having a career closely related to her core purpose, and also being able to have peak volunteer experiences also aligned with her purpose.

"In 1961, I graduated from McGill with a baccalaureate in nursing and had an opportunity to go to Africa with an organization that provided opportunities for young people to volunteer," she said. "This was in the days when apartheid was still very strong. I think that was when my eyes were first opened and I realized then that the world was a lot bigger than that little part of Canada I was from. That spurred my interest in understanding the needs of others, particularly in the developing world." That trip to Africa turned out to be one of a number of peak experiences in Dawn's life over the next fifty years.

It's interesting, looking back at Dawn's life, to see how she moved forward from the experience of losing her husband and parents, relocating her family, and trying to find a way to provide for them. She did not shrink back into what little Comfort Zone she had left. A pattern emerged, both in her career and in her volunteer experiences, which has eventually included leadership roles serving as past chair of the Peterborough Hospital Board, chairing a Peterborough United Way fund-raising campaign, working her way up through the executive positions in her local Rotary Club, and eventually becoming the District Governor for her Rotary District. Every time Dawn got involved in something, she ended up chairing it or leading it in some way.

When asked why this was the case, Dawn's response was a humble one. "I don't know why," she said. "Maybe it's because I'm a detail person. When I sit on a board, I work on it as though it was a job and try to be there as much as I can."

It became evident throughout our interview with Dawn that she may just be one of those natural leaders who volunteer tirelessly for the organization she is involved with at that time. What was also evident was her commitment to spend part of her time in the Lifeworth Zone—being there on-purpose. At the time of our interview, at age seventy-one, Dawn was the District Governor of Rotary for District 7010, which includes central and northern Ontario and north-west Quebec. To be recommended for this position, Dawn had to have passed through the various executive positions at the local level.

"I have had the opportunity to travel and help people in other parts of the world, particularly through Rotary," Dawn said. "One of the more recent Rotary projects has been the distribution of wheelchairs to Third World countries. I've been on five of these trips and led the last three. In 2008, we took 1,400 brand new wheelchairs to El Salvador, where we have built some lasting relationships with people there. On other recent trips, we delivered 260 and 540 wheelchairs to needy children and adults in Jamaica and Equador. To assist with the chair distribution on these service/awareness trips, I was accompanied by twenty-two fellow Rotarians and partners to Jamaica and twenty-eight to Ecuador. The response was tremendous! Most of them declared that their time away was life-altering.

"I find being involved interesting and challenging. I'm always trying to find new and somewhat different experiences that I feel I'm capable of doing. I like to do different things, to be challenged, and most important, to help others meet some of their basic needs."

As we probed further, it became apparent Dawn continues to seek out different types of peak experiences, to seek ways to feel enriched in her life. When asked how she would describe *Lifeworth* and how she would motivate others to pursue their life worth living, Dawn provided us with some very sage advice.

"I encourage people, even my boys, to take advantage of any opportunity to enrich themselves beyond their current horizon; to enrich themselves beyond where they are at," she said. "I believe that one has to serve one's own community, as well as other parts of the world." Dawn has gone outside of her Comfort Zone throughout her life to donate her time and enrich the lives of others.

"Don't limit yourself," Dawn said when asked for her advice for people struggling to escape their own Comfort Zone. "Don't be afraid. I would encourage people to step outside of their Comfort Zone and to challenge their horizons. If you aren't sure where to turn to or how to volunteer, look for something that has some meaning to you. If you don't get involved with something that has meaning to you, you might lose interest. Start somewhere and, if that doesn't work out, use it as a learning experience to find the next situation that might fit you better. Trying different volunteer opportunities might help you find out what your values and purpose might be."

Dawn did not shrink back into whatever Comfort Zone she had left after the death of her husband and parents, peak experiences in their own right. She had to eventually let go of the fear of being a single parent, of wondering if she could support her family, of what her future held for her. She moved to Peterborough, found an engaging career in the human services sector that allowed her to use her skills and passion for helping others, and made the most of many volunteer opportunities. Like Jeanelle and Susan, Dawn's desire to seek out new challenges that could help others couldn't help but pull her into her future and different peak experiences, for the most part, within her own community. ∎

For more information about Jeanelle's cookbook, see
www.loveofsoup.com

SO NOW WHAT?

These three stories illustrate how we can create peak experiences, helping us move in and out of our Lifeworth Zones during the course of our lives. These women did so without making huge transitions in their lives. Each time they reached out to help others, they created a peak experience within their Lifeworth Zone. They used the marbles they had in their marble bags at the time.

- What Time, Talent, or Treasure Marbles do you have in your bag right now?

- With the marbles you have right now, can you identify one volunteer opportunity to create a peak experience in your Lifeworth Zone? A volunteer opportunity in an area that you think would be fulfilling or rewarding?

- How could you use your marbles to move out of your Comfort Zone and help others in need?

- Write this down and tack it up where you can see it every day.

CHAPTER TEN

BREAKING THROUGH
THE WALL

One can choose to go back toward safety
or forward toward growth.
Growth must be chosen again and again;
fear must be overcome again and again.

ABRAHAM MASLOW

Your exploration through this book so far has introduced you to a different perspective of the Comfort Zone, a new concept called the Lifeworth Zone, a description of peak experiences, and the concept of Free Reining. We have even given you a hint of a type of "wall" that could act as a barrier between the Comfort Zone and the Lifeworth Zone. This wall is shown in Figure 10.1. In this chapter, we will explore the concept of the wall in more depth and provide you with some insights and examples of how to break through your own wall into a peak experience in the Lifeworth Zone.

Many of us have heard of the wall in terms of the runner's wall, the psychological wall that long-distance runners may hit at some point during a race. Those who prepare for it and who push through it find a newfound sense of freedom and ability to complete the run. If you are a runner, you may have experienced this feeling.

Have you ever had to speak at a public event? You practice your speech relentlessly, envisioning yourself in front of the audience, and then it is time for you to deliver the goods. As you walk to the podium, you might hit another type of wall, one of fear and nervousness. "Can I do this? I can't remember my speech! What will people think?"

Have you ever refused to try or take part in something because you felt it was outside of your Comfort Zone? The wall we are referring to is the wall that confines us to our Comfort Zone. It is the wall that separates the Comfort Zone from the Lifeworth Zone, as shown Figure 10.1, below.

Figure 10.1

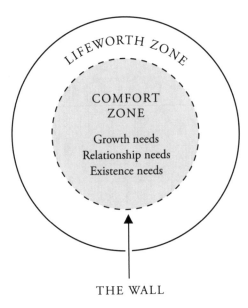

THE WALL

It can be a wall of fear, of uncertainty, of not knowing what lies on the other side (in other words, our future). It can be a psychological wall, sometimes of Herculean proportions, that keeps us on this side. Or, it can be a more physical, tangible wall—like the runner's wall—where we don't know if we have enough energy left. We may not have enough Treasure Marbles, or we can't seem to find enough Time Marbles. We may think we don't have the Talent Marbles or the ability, or we may wonder what others will think of us if we fail.

It is an invisible, but all-too-real wall within all of us to some degree. When we see this wall in our mind, we begin to pull back on the "bits in our mouth." Although we didn't use the term "wall" in Chapter 7, we introduced the concept when we said, "Fear is the great crippler; lack of confidence is the great inhibitor." We talked about how we all have some type of bit in our mouth, holding us back from moving into different areas of our lives, just like a horse's bit prevents it from wandering off on its own.

Some type of wall, however small or large, appears every time we face a decision. Some decisions are so small or everyday in nature that we don't even notice the bit. For example, deciding what colour shirt to wear, or what restaurant or movie we want to go to. In these circumstances, creating "slack in the reins," so to speak, isn't difficult and we just get on with it. We go through everyday mini-walls of decision quite easily, because we have developed thinking patterns for doing so.

However, some decisions are much more difficult. The walls they create can be more intimidating. We feel the pull of the bit in our mouth as we review that wall in our mind. It is almost as if we had an inexperienced rider hauling back hard on the reins out of fear and lack of confidence. "Don't let that horse go too fast!" We procrastinate. We find excuses for not following through. The bit and the wall are connected to each other. We recognize the wall whenever it appears in our lives, and our first instinct is to pull back on the bit, to not go too fast, or to completely stop moving in that direction. For example, if a new job opportunity suddenly presents itself our initial reaction might be to pull back on the reins and say, "Whoa! Where did that come from? Can I do this? Am I prepared for this? Do I have enough Talent Marbles to take this on?" This type of decision represents a bigger wall that may create fear and anxiety. This is not an everyday decision for which we have developed thinking patterns to handle. Breaking Through the Wall begins by recognizing that we want to do something different with our lives, or act on something we have thought about for some time. But, for many reasons, or, due to our own excuses, we have not managed to make that change. In order to Break Through the Wall, we have to make a start at doing something different. After all, Breaking Through the Wall is about making a change in your life, moving from the comfort of "here and now" to the uncertainty of "out there." We make many attempts to move forward, usually beginning by *starting* to do something different, something new. And it is right here, at the start, that most of us miss the mark.

William Bridges, in his book, *Transitions: Making Sense of Life's Changes*, refers to "transition" as the psychological aspects that are related to the physical outcomes of "change." Transition relates to the emotions that are going on internally beneath the surface while the physical change is taking place externally. For example, if you have ever moved your family from one house to another, or if you remember when you left your parents' house to live in your own place, change refers to the packing, moving, and unpacking of all your belongings. It involves moving from one physical building to another. Transition, on the other hand, refers to the emotions and thoughts of leaving the experiences and memories of the old home behind and beginning to make psychological adjustments to a new place and starting to develop new experiences and memories.

It is the transition or psychological aspect of Breaking Through the Wall that we explore in this chapter. Bridges recognized that the first part of any transition is not the process of beginning to do something, but rather it's the process of stopping to do certain things. We need to let go of emotional attachments or fears that hold us back from moving out of our Comfort Zone and into a peak experience in the Lifeworth Zone. In order for us to loosen the reins and take the pressure off the bit so that we can Free Rein, we actually have to let go of the reins. In order for us to start the process of Breaking Through the Wall, we have to recognize in ourselves those things that are holding us back; these are the "bits" in our minds. We can make many starts, but, inevitably, we tend to revert back to the old ways of doing things. How many times have you tried to lose weight, to stop smoking, to eat healthier, to manage your time better, to save for a longer vacation, to learn a new skill? We can become afraid and confused. We can procrastinate, lose focus, and our survival instincts kick in. As human beings, we are instinctively programmed for keeping things normal, constant, and comfortable. Any change in our surroundings or in our environment causes us to take notice and try to return things to normal. It initiates a stress or anxiety response. The Comfort Zone suddenly becomes a bit more comfortable than we thought it was. In the examples above, many people achieve their goals of losing weight, stopping smoking, eating healthier, managing their time, saving for a nice vacation, or learning a new skill. They successfully make the transition to a new way of living or of achieving their goals. But many don't. Understanding this process will help you achieve your desired peak experience.

Let's consider this concept by using a couple of common, everyday rubber bands. Picture two identical rubber bands lying on a table. Even better, put down the book and actually get two rubber bands of the same length and thickness. We'll wait for you.

Now, pick up one of the rubber bands and hold it lightly between your two thumbs (Figure 10.2). Your left thumb represents where you are today in your Comfort Zone, and your right thumb represents where you would like to go, the peak experience you would like to achieve in the Lifeworth Zone.

Figure 10.2

If you move your right thumb away from your left one while holding your left thumb steady, the rubber band begins to stretch and resist. In a simplistic sort of way, this is how our minds are programmed. Something is changing, and we initially want to take the pressure off by returning back to our Comfort Zone. This is perfectly normal! We have all done it, and we will all continue to do it at different times in our lives. Now, stretch the rubber band between your thumbs to its fullest extension, without breaking it. You can feel the increasing pressure in the band to return to normal, to stop stretching. Slowly release the rubber band, and then place it on the table next to the other band you have not yet picked up. You will notice the stretched rubber band is now somewhat longer than the unstretched one. Although all of the pressure is off, the rubber band could not return to its original size. Our lives are like that. Every time we stretch ourselves out of our Comfort Zone, even a little bit, we grow and learn new things about ourselves, and nothing can undo this. We can use and build on this new knowledge in our next attempt to stretch our limits or to Break Through the Wall.

Let's go back to the rubber bands. Take the one you originally stretched and put it between your left and right thumbs again. And, once again, pull your right thumb slowly to the right, while still holding your left thumb steady. You are moving toward your peak experience. Again, you will feel the elastic pressure building, trying to pull that right thumb back. By now, you should have the rubber band stretched to its maximum limit without breaking. At least two uncertainties exist now: *how long* you can hold the rubber band at maximum stretch before you tire, and *how far* you can go before it breaks, causing one of your thumbs to feel a bit of pain from the snapback of the broken band. Okay, let's remove the uncertainty. Stretch the rubber band until it breaks. Keep going—come on—make it break! Did it hurt?

Hopefully, you didn't pick a thick rubber band for this experiment. The first time Dana did this with a group of financial advisors that he coaches, he gave them a choice of rubber bands of different thicknesses and lengths. Some chose thinner ones, and some chose the thicker ones. Ever watch six grown men slowly stretching rubber bands until they break? It's not pretty! Looks of apprehension, heads turned to the side, an eye or two closed, a grimace of anticipation of the impending pain! Ever listen to them after it breaks? Sorry, we can't repeat some of the comments here!

Breaking the rubber band is similar to Breaking Through the Wall. It might take lots of time, energy, or attempts to actually make it through, but, then, you're there, achieving your peak experience. Breaking Through the Wall is about execution. It is about the execution of our peak experiences and it is the heart of this book. It involves three general zones or phases: letting go of the Comfort Zone, moving through a zone of uncertainty, and achieving a peak experience in the Lifeworth Zone. Have a look at Figure 10.3.

Figure 10.3

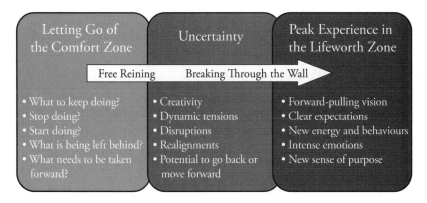

Letting Go of the Comfort Zone	Uncertainty	Peak Experience in the Lifeworth Zone
Free Reining	Breaking Through the Wall	
• What to keep doing? • Stop doing? • Start doing? • What is being left behind? • What needs to be taken forward?	• Creativity • Dynamic tensions • Disruptions • Realignments • Potential to go back or move forward	• Forward-pulling vision • Clear expectations • New energy and behaviours • Intense emotions • New sense of purpose

Although the process flows from left to right, we actually need to start the process at the right-hand side. We have to clearly define what peak experience we want to achieve outside of our Comfort Zone. It may be a twenty-fifth anniversary vacation, or hiking a trail that has seemed too difficult until now, or learning to play a new musical instrument, or volunteering for the first time, or many other possibilities. You will need to ask yourself questions such as:

- What peak experience do I want to achieve?

- What will the experience feel like, physically and emotionally?

- Why do I want to do this?

- What resources (or marbles) do I need?

- When will I do it?

- Should I or could I share this experience with someone else?

Take some time to envision how you could add additional fulfillment to your life, a truly fulfilling peak experience. Here are further questions to ask yourself:

- What did you want to be when you grew up?

- What have you always wanted to do that you haven't done yet?

- What have you done in your life that you are really proud of?

- What brings you the most fulfillment and how does this relate to your Time, Talent, and Treasure Marbles?

Tune in to the emotions you could experience from your peak experience. Without emotions, many peak experiences may not happen. You can write the pros and cons on paper, weigh them back and forth, and look at them logically from all sides. But it's your emotions that will cause you to take action, to take those first tentative steps into the Uncertainty Zone. Your emotions will provide you with that irrational leap of faith that says, "Okay, let's do this!" Try to tap into some of the emotions you may have experienced from past peak experiences. Try to imagine and almost feel the emotions of a future peak experience. The point here is to create a strong mental and emotional vision of your potential peak experience. If you want, find some pictures or words that vividly illustrate or describe your potential experience. Put them where you can see them and be reminded of the peak experience you are planning. The goal is to make that image so strong, so desirable, that it will pull you into the future. The desire for a peak experience should be a forward-pulling vision of what you are trying to achieve. You will develop new knowledge, new energy, and a new sense of purpose.

Great! We are assuming by now you have some type of peak experience clearly in mind. So, let's get started. On the left side of the chart, we begin the process of Free Reining and thinking about Breaking Through the Wall to achieve the peak experience we have defined. That is when we start to encounter the bits in our mouth; the fears that could be holding us back. When we start Free Reining, we have to let go of some of these bits. Unlike a horse, we can have multiple bits that can control our efforts because these bits exist in our minds. Fear is one of the bits that can hold us back. But there are different types of fears. We have to identify and address any specific fears. For example, the fear of failure is one type of bit. Ask yourself why you are afraid of failing. Are you afraid of disappointing yourself or someone else? Remember that Tom Droog was more afraid of disappointing his wife, Emmy, than himself. Fear of being hurt emotionally or physically is another type of bit. Identify the potential risks involved and figure out how to reduce or eliminate them. Are they real or perceived risks? Ask yourself, "What's the worst that could happen?"

In the Comfort Zone on the left of Figure 10.3, we need to ask ourselves the following questions:

- What do I need to keep doing?

- What do I need to stop doing?

- What do I need to start doing?

- What is being left behind?

- What needs to be taken forward with me?

Since we are trying to create a peak experience outside of our Comfort Zone in the Lifeworth Zone, here are some additional questions to ask:

- Are you receiving fulfillment, satisfaction, and value in proportion to how you are spending your marbles in your Comfort Zone?

- Is the expenditure of your marbles in alignment with what you value, what you are passionate about, and what you believe your life purpose is at this point in your life?

- How would you use your marbles differently if you didn't have to work for a living?

Once we have answered these questions, and have identified what could be holding us back, we can ease the pressure from the bits in our mouth. Free Reining takes us into the Uncertainty Zone.

The Uncertainty Zone in the middle can be an area of creativity, opportunity, disruption, stress, and fear, all at the same time. We begin to experience a dynamic tension between the forward pull of our desire to achieve the peak experience and the backward pull of returning to the Comfort Zone. In the Uncertainty Zone, there is the potential to go back or to move forward. This is the rubber band being stretched out. The bits are pulling us back into the Comfort Zone, and the challenge and desire for the peak experience are pulling us forward. Forward, backward. Future, present. Confidence, lack of confidence. Fear, no fear. Pulled one way, then the other.

This is the zone where we might start to experience a sense of exhilaration, a sense of moving forward, a sense of being able to create a new challenge or opportunity for ourselves. It is also an area where we can begin to feel a sense of disruption and trepidation. Are we going in the right direction? Do we have what it takes to pull this off? This is also where we begin to feel the pull of various bits, the fears or questions in our mind.

In the Uncertainty Zone, you need to go back and ask yourself the same questions you answered when you started to Free Rein in the Comfort Zone. Make sure you are letting go of anything that could be holding you back. Make sure you know what skills and resources you need. What marbles do you need in your marble bag? Can you redistribute some of the marbles if necessary, or do you have to collect some new Talent or Treasure Marbles? Remind yourself that part of the Free Reining process is developing any new skills (Talent Marbles) you might need to move toward your peak experience.

As well, you also need to take time to reflect on and clarify what you are trying to achieve. What do you want this peak experience to be? If there were no obstacles at all, and you could create the best peak experience possible, what would it look like? How would it feel? What emotions would you feel? How will the achievement feel when it is completed? The clearer your answers are to these types of questions, the stronger the pull of the peak experience into the Lifeworth Zone.

Here's a quick analogy for you to try. You will need a piece of string approximately three feet (about 90 centimetres) long; a shoelace, a rope, a piece of yarn, or a ribbon will also work. Lay the string out from end to end in a straight line on a surface. Now take one end of the string and try to push the far end and the entire string forward while keeping it straight at the same time. You'll probably need to actually try this to get the full impact. Go ahead. Try it!

So, how did you make out? Could you do it? In most cases, the string will begin to bend in different directions before the other end even starts to move. There are a lot of variables affecting the process: the thickness of the string, the type of surface it is on, what the string is made of, and how hard or fast you try to push it. But that's okay; there are a lot of similar variables in the game of life. Want to try it again with a new variable? Straighten out your string on the surface again. This time, instead of pushing from one end, try grasping the string at about the mid-point and start the forward push from there. What did you notice? Did the forward half of the string start to bend in different directions? Did you manage to push the far end of the string forward, at least a little bit? What about the piece of string that was behind your fingers and being pulled forward? Did it bend, or did it just come along in a straight line? We're guessing it did.

What happens to the entire experiment if we take the leading end of the string and pull the entire string forward, with no pushing at all? Now you are making progress! You are pulling all of the string forward in a relatively straight line, right to where you want the string to go.

The pull of our future peak experience should feel like being pulled into your future, as with the piece of string. You can't wait to get there and experience it! It should be strong enough to overcome the various obstacles you encounter along the journey, the same types of obstacles that could be causing the string to bend as you tried to push it. Think of it this way: are you trying to push your way out of your Comfort Zone, or are you being pulled into the Lifeworth Zone by your desire to achieve your peak experience? If you are pushing, it is much more difficult to let go of the different bits in your mouth. You may still have some fear and trepidation holding you back as you take tentative, timid steps forward. If you are being pulled, it is much easier to let go of each bit as it begins to pull on your mind, because you are anchored in the future. Tap into your emotions. They won't push you blindly into your future. They will pull you into it with purpose and direction. You have made the full commitment to achieving the peak experience and are taking powerful, purposeful steps into the Lifeworth Zone.

Once you Break Through the Wall on the right of Figure 10.3, you will know it. Like Lindsay Sears, you may experience the first-hand impact you had on someone in need. Like Katy Hutchison (in the next chapter), you may experience knowing you have made the right decision. Like Paul Henderson (in Chapter 12), you might feel a "true and lasting inner peace that comes from a deep commitment." Like Tom Droog, the experience may "feel good in your gut." Like John Davidson or Martha Birkett, you might feel the exhilaration of completing a physically demanding journey. You will know it; you will feel it. ∎

SO NOW WHAT?

In this chapter, we hope we have given you a new perspective on how to break out of your Comfort Zone. We hope we have provided you with questions that help you find answers to whatever might be keeping you from Breaking Through the Wall into the Lifeworth Zone.

• What fears or uncertainties, or lack of marbles, are the "bits" in your mouth holding you back? Make a list of them; put them on paper so you can see them and question them. If you didn't do this at the end of Chapter 7, do it now. Letting go is a key part of the process.

- Is your peak experience strong and clear in your mind? What is so engaging about this peak experience that you can feel its pull?

- What emotions can you associate with your peak experience to increase its pull on you? Imagine what emotions you would like to feel. Think back to emotions you felt in previous peak experiences.

- Take time to go back and review the questions related to "Letting Go in the Comfort Zone" and to "Achieving a Peak Experience in the Lifeworth Zone" in this chapter. Write down your answers. Share them with someone so that they can help keep you accountable and moving forward.

CHAPTER ELEVEN

THE "F" WORD

—KATY HUTCHISON

Forgiveness does not change the past,
but it does enlarge the future.

PAUL BOESE

Katy Hutchison of Victoria, British Columbia, was referred to us by Tim Mitchell and Michael Diamond, both of Toronto. Katy Hutchison's story is one of heartache and triumph. Her life path was, initially, what she had planned for herself: marrying Bob McIntosh, having children (Emma and Sam), and living in a respected Vancouver neighbourhood. Life was good. But on New Year's Eve 1997, all that changed when Bob decided to go up the street to check out a loud house party that seemed out of control.

In a haze of alcohol and drugs, the youth at the party, including a twenty-year-old man named Ryan, ganged up on Bob and began beating him. Bob died of his wounds that same evening. Life for everyone involved that night changed forever. Emma and Sam, then only four, lost a father; Katy lost a husband; and the killer would live with his mistake for the rest of his life.

In 1998, Katy met her future husband, Michael Hutchison, her lawyer through the course of the legal proceedings, and has been happily married to him for the past thirteen years. She has started a new life in Victoria, and the twins, eighteen years old at the time of this interview, are doing very well. Although it was a long and difficult road at first, Katy turned something ugly into something truly inspirational. She recounted the events of that tragic night in her best-selling book, *Walking After Midnight,* which formed the basis of the Lifetime Network film *Bond of Silence.* Katy is a sought-after speaker throughout North America, primarily presenting to schools, youth and parent groups, and justice groups. Both she and Michael work with Leave Out Violence (LOVE), an organization formed in 1993 by victims of crime. Its purpose is to educate Canadian youth to eliminate violence in schools and everyday life.

Katy believes that how you react to events in your life is even more important than what actually happens to you. Here is Katy in her own words.

● ● ● ●

There is something I want to share with you. I was speaking at a large international conference last year where the analogy of a river came up. All the legal practitioners in attendance were coming from different tributaries, but were meeting together into a common stream, with a common purpose.

Most of the people in that room had chosen to be in that river. They had gone to school and studied criminology and law. They had become practitioners in law or justice. They had chosen a field of study and, here they were, meeting with commonality. I had not planned to be in that room. I wouldn't have thought my life would have taken such a drastic turn that I would find myself at this conference, in their common river. I felt like I had actually leapt from a falls to be in their river. We just never know how people come to be in certain places in their lives.

The people in that room may have looked at me, not knowing a lot about my background, and said, "Hey, she seems successful and living every day with intention." But how did I get there? What forces pushed me in their direction?

Flashing back thirteen years, I literally had an "ah-ha" moment standing in the hospital, watching the EMTs and the doctors trying to resuscitate my husband. Everybody in that room—the doctors, the nurses, and the police—were all doing what they had been trained to do as professionals at a time of crisis. But there was really only one person in the room who was going to have to get up the next day and carry on—and that was me. I wasn't at work. My shift wasn't going to just end and, the next day, life would not go on as usual.

It was at that moment that I felt this wash of emotion and light flood across me. I had a real sense of having to choose who I was going to be. When the doctors finally came out of the emergency room and I received the news that Bob hadn't made it, that he was gone, I felt like I was going to collapse. I heard this sound—this deep, guttural sound—and then realized that the sound was coming from me. I thought, "I don't want to be that person." I didn't want to be the single mom wondering "where to from here?" I couldn't be. I had two four year-olds at home who thought they were going to be getting up the next day to build a snowman, not launching into a period that no child should ever have to live through.

It was at that moment I realized that I couldn't control what had just happened. At that point, I really didn't know what happened at that party. All I knew was that Bob was gone. Like that, in a flash, our lives had changed. For some people, the feeling of needing to take control comes much later but, for me, it was right away. I realized right then and there that I could still pick the person I was going to be. It was still my choice. That hadn't been taken away from me.

Who was I going to be? How was I going to handle one second to the next, because, at that point, it was just second to second? Gradually, it became minute to minute, hour to hour, then day to day. I had always held on to the belief that, although there was a lot that I couldn't control, I could control how I was going to respond and how I was going to move forward. I didn't know how, but I did come to the strong realization and commitment that I could decide. Not society. Not the media. Just me. As hard as it might be, I knew someone had to drive the bus—and it was really my bus to drive.

And the need to take some degree of control was immediate, because, only about twenty-four hours later, a reporter asked me what I wanted to see happen to the person who killed Bob. I felt sick to my stomach when I heard the question, because I knew what I was about to say was not going to sit well with some of my family, friends, and the general public. I felt people were going to want me to say that I wanted to see the person in jail for the rest of his life. An eye for an eye. But that was not how I was feeling. I wanted to know that the person or the people were going to be okay. I wanted to know what had happened. I was more interested in what the precursors to the event were so that we could do everything we could as a community so that this didn't happen again.

This was a situation where Bob merely went up the street because there was a noisy house party. He wasn't mugged by somebody with a sordid criminal history. This was a bunch of kids having fun and it got out of control. I knew he had gone to the party, but for the longest time, we had to assume what had happened. We didn't have any specific details of the people at the party or the events leading up to Bob's murder. All we knew is that he walked into a party and didn't come out again. It all happened extremely quickly. I kept wondering, what's going on in our community that a party could get so out of control? What were we going to do so that we didn't repeat this situation?

That journey of finding out what happened and making an arrest took five years. The police were patient and diligent in their undercover work. If you are interested in learning more of the details surrounding the party,

Bob's murder, and the subsequent arrest years later, there is a lot of detail in the book I wrote about this, *Walking After Midnight.*

My participation in Hal and Dana's book, *Lifeworth,* is not so much about what happened to me and my children, but more about what I have done with my life since, how I have dedicated my life to helping others through their dark days, helping at-risk children, helping people deal with stress, failure, abuse, and heartache. Helping others rise up in their lives after life has dealt them a serious blow or setback. Helping people to regain some degree of control and sense of normalcy in their lives.

For me, part of taking my life back and driving my own bus was to immediately leave Vancouver and my old neighbourhood. We have real conventions in our North American society about what is appropriate to do after a loss. Everyone will say not to make any major changes or decisions for twelve months. Well, who wrote that book? For me, why would I stay? What on Earth was there for me when there was an unsolved murder and I had family and friends in Victoria, where I had grown up? So I immediately moved.

I think the next brave thing I did that flies in the face of what people think is right is, even though I was grieving, I fell in love. I think of all the parts of the story that are important, really human, and will touch people reading *Lifeworth,* it was allowing myself to fall in love again. So many people don't. Michael and I have been married for thirteen years and so many people said I was crazy.

No one will ever walk in my shoes and I will never be in anyone else's. The piece I'd like people to take away is, yes, there was a lot happening in a short period of time but, when I look at our kids now, all the trauma and change happened within a year. By the time they were five and in kindergarten, their lives were back to a semblance of normal. I look at my own mom who lost her husband, my dad, in 1985. She never remarried. I think part of the reason people don't move on is they expect one day they are going to wake up and the grief is going to magically be gone, that there is going to be some kind of sign that they are ready to move forward. That sign is never going to come. People have to make decisions.

I'll always have a place in my heart to grieve for Bob, but that didn't mean that I wasn't going to allow myself to fall in love with Michael. And just that little piece of permission is so critical. So many men and women have come to me after my presentations, where they thought that they were going to be listening to a piece on drug and alcohol safety for teenagers, and they've come away saying that this permission-granting was the part that really hit them.

We're talking about loss, real loss that everyday people are experiencing each day. My sister's husband left her after thirty years of marriage, right after Bob was killed. We basically had parallel journeys. In some ways, hers was more complicated because she still had to deal with him. My situation was more immediate. When things are so traumatic and instant, like a murder, perhaps the adjustment to a new way of life requires a more immediate focus.

My mom died recently, after battling cancer for a year. Watching somebody disappear a teaspoon at a time is very difficult. I suppose the silver in the lining, though, is that at least a person has time to remember the good times and say goodbye.

For the next few years, Michael and I built a life together. Michael was my rock and truly helped me in the healing and grieving process. He allowed me the time to reflect, as well as to look forward in life. I have been lucky and blessed with two very loving men in my life. So lucky.

Because no one was coming forward, I got busy with raising a family, remarrying, and re-establishing myself in a new community. I just waited for the police to do what they needed to do and tried my best to carve out a new life for myself, knowing things were going to be very different.

And then one day, I finally received the call I had hoped for. It was from the police department. Five years after Bob's murder, they were ready to make an arrest. No one had come forward all these years. There was this code of silence in the community. I said my intention was to find the person responsible, but that I hoped the person was okay.

I shocked the police by telling them I was on my way. They said, "What do you mean?" I said I wanted to be there. I needed to meet the guy. I had some questions and I knew that wasn't going to take place in a courtroom. I knew that the police were just shaking their heads thinking, she's crazy. But why would you not want to sit down with the person who killed a loved one? I thought, who better than me to sit down and ask the tough questions? The police didn't really know what to do, so they let me come in.

I was in the interrogation room waiting for him to walk through the door and I'm sure that my mind was conjuring up all kinds of images of some monster. And then this young man walks through the door, a young man who could be your son or the boy next door. I realized that society creates a huge gap between us and the people who cause us harm. So when I saw him and realized that he was somebody's child, that gap got real small in a heck of a hurry.

Hal and Dana asked me to describe a peak experience I might have had in my life. Meeting Ryan for the first time was definitely one. The emotions for both of us were quite high. Each of us wondering how this meeting might go. Ryan wondering what my reaction and attitude might be. But when I met him, I calmly asked him some tough questions. Ryan was now twenty-five and had been living with the fact that he had taken another person's life and changed both our families forever. What a burden to have carried for someone so young. But, although my heart was filling with a growing sense of compassion as we spoke, I did say, "Don't you dare put my family or your own family through a trial. Plead guilty and let's get on with this." And so he did. We dispensed with a long court process and I promised him that I would stand by him to make sure that he received the help he needed through the system.

Once Ryan was incarcerated, I was worried about what was going to happen to him in jail. I knew enough about the criminal justice program to know that there was a good chance he was going to come out worse than when he'd gone in. So I took it upon myself to learn about alternative ways of dealing with punishment in serious cases, and to pursue the whole notion of restorative justice. That was really the formal name for what I helped achieve by sitting down with Ryan in the first place. Bringing the victims and the offenders together to talk about how it has affected both sides, as well as the community, is so important to the healing process. It's how we move forward and create safe communities.

For Ryan, there wasn't any sort of glaring incident in his life that would lead people to think he could end up killing someone. There were a few things that people might have said were pretty typical. His parents split up when he was in Grade 5 and he felt that pull from one tent to the other. Who do I live with? Ryan was a little bit smaller than his classmates and had a speech impediment. These are all little things that we see around us all the time but, layered one on top of the other, compounded with a propensity not to communicate, to be a withdrawn child, they led him to a place in life where getting drunk and putting his fist through a wall was the release he was looking for. Sadly, it wasn't a wall Ryan's fist went through the night Bob was killed.

As a result of all this, I became very interested in how normal families and normal children, your average everyday Canadian family, can find themselves in a situation where people like Ryan can do what they do. I thought Bob and Ryan's story definitely needed to be told, somehow, somewhere. So I contacted the high school in Victoria that I had attended and I said, "I know kids are getting a lot of messages around social responsibility and drinking and driving, but what about all the other things that happen when kids get drunk, such as unprotected sex, bullying, and fights at parties? Who talks about that?" Nobody talks about that. So that's how my new mission in life was born. Bob's murder was now solved, and I was actively trying to help Ryan through his jail time, his repayment to society, and to help him start the rest of his life on the right foot.

Now I wasn't just looking to the past. I was able to firmly look to the future with a renewed sense of purpose by helping take such an ugly event and possibly turn it into something positive. It wasn't so much just sharing my story. I felt as though I was put in this place to help create a safe place for others to consider their own life experiences and how they can reframe themselves.

Each time I speak to a school group, many young men come up to me after a presentation and ask to speak to me in private, away from the crowd, and say to me, "I could be Ryan. I'm that kid. What do I do now? How do I get the help that I need?" Oftentimes, girls will come up to me and say, "I'm dating 'Ryan.'" And to this day, I'm still puzzled and amazed as to how we as a society arrive at the point where some—not all—of our youth are turning out this way.

In the parent workshops that I do, one of the things that I warn parents about is the over-programmed child. The kid that is always on his way to the next practice, the next event, the next commitment, being constantly challenged and put out there. I encourage families to just unplug and hang out. The best times the four of us in my family have had together are those over-dinner conversations that went on for two hours, leaning up against the kitchen counter, just hanging out and being together—not always being on our way to somewhere else.

In 2009, our daughter, Emma, did an exchange in South Africa for ten weeks. The family she stayed with had her travelling all over the country with them. She saw everything. She had an incredible experience. Then they sent their daughter back to us in Victoria for the months of January to

March. It rained the entire time and there wasn't enough snow on the mountains to go skiing. The way the timing worked out, there weren't a lot of holiday days. So we didn't have an opportunity to do a lot of things outside the home. At the end of the experience, I asked her how she had enjoyed Canada and, of course, one of the really unique things for her was to be able to walk down to the corner store instead of being in an armed vehicle. However, she said her most remarkable memory of being in Canada was that we sat down as a family and had dinner together almost every night. To travel halfway around the world to eat meatballs, who would have thought? She said they don't do that [in South Africa] and, here in Canada, it's becoming less and less common. We have to reverse that.

To use Hal and Dana's terms, I try to encourage parents to live a life worth living and to set that great example for their children. We all get busy with hectic schedules and commitments from time to time, but slowing down is as essential in life as speeding up. Taking the time to look inward, not outward. Setting priorities and goals that come from within. I think one of the bravest things a person can do is look inward. It takes guts to be honest with ourselves. As a society, we're constantly looking for external stimuli. Take the time to train yourself to look inward every day, or as much as you can.

I encourage every person I speak with to live life with maximum engagement. We should describe where we want to be in life by using adjectives. Rather than making a New Year's resolution to lose ten pounds, try to articulate and write down how it would feel if you lost ten pounds. It's the feeling that should be the goal and then it becomes more achievable and sustainable. So the *Lifeworth* advice here is getting to know yourself well enough to know what situations are going to elicit that real feeling of engagement and belonging.

My story has not come from a place of faith. So much that is written about family comes from a faith angle and that is great for people who celebrate their faith. But some people have a different experience and don't necessarily define it in a faith-based way. Each situation is different, not right or wrong. I do a workshop on the "F" word, on *forgiveness*. As soon as you say the word forgiveness, it conjures up all kinds of connotations and one of them comes from a place of faith. For me, it was about being practical. Forgiveness was my way of being able to move on and have a life. It was being okay with letting go of a future that wasn't going to happen. It was enabling me to not be defined by what happened to Bob. I would much rather be defined by the relationship that I *am* in, not by the relationship I *was* in. Not by one moment that fateful New Year's Eve over which I had no control.

So forgiveness was imperative, and it wasn't just about forgiving Ryan as much as it was about forgiving the situation. I extended forgiveness to him, but I needed to forgive myself, too. I think that was the thing. It also required some self-forgiveness because I chose to move on quickly and do things that people were critical of. I had to forgive myself for being okay with that and saying, "No, this is the way I'm going to do this." It was, and is, my life.

I've always been an emotional risk-taker. I think if I were to leave you with one thing, it would be as simple as encouraging you to examine your own relationship with yourself and your family. It all comes down to relationships. Whether you're talking about your networth or your *Lifeworth*, what is going to wind into that tapestry is going to be relationships with yourself and with those around you. Learn to use and practice the "F" word. Embed that into your psyche. Make it a part of your everyday life. Learn to forgive yourself. Look inward, not outward, and learn to forgive others. You'll then live your life more fully engaged, fully alive, and ready for anything that life can throw at you. Anything. ∎

To learn about Katy's experiences, visit www.katyhutchisonpresents.com

SO NOW WHAT?

Katy has provided some great examples of Breaking Through the Wall after she was thrust into an intensely emotional situation following Bob's murder. She took that one unplanned, heart-wrenching peak experience and turned it into several well-thought-out, positive peak experiences. She said early in her story that, although she couldn't control the circumstances around her, she could choose how she responded to them and how she chose to move forward. She told us that the sign to move forward or to change usually never just comes to us. People have to make decisions to take action. Katy indicated that we need to permit ourselves to move forward in life, to let go of what might be holding us back. Her *Lifeworth* advice was "getting to know yourself well enough to know what situations are going to elicit that feeling of engagement and belonging."

These are all key aspects of Breaking Through the Wall: controlling how we respond to the situations around us, making decisions to take action, giving ourselves permission to achieve a peak experience, and knowing ourselves well enough to clearly and emotionally define our peak experience so that it pulls us into the future.

- Have you had a negative peak experience in your life that was unplanned, that was thrust upon you when life was going along just as you had planned?

- How did you, or can you, turn that experience into a positive, well-thought-out peak experience?

- Are there situations that you perceive as barriers, challenges, or fears to achieving your peak experience? Can you change how you think about them and how you respond to them to reduce their impact on your journey?

- Make a list of the first few decisions you need to make in order to achieve your peak experience. What decisions can be made in the next day, week, or month? Create a sense of urgency around your decisions to motivate you to take action.

- Is the peak experience you have in mind clearly and closely related to who you are or who you would like to be? Is it strong enough to motivate you into taking action sooner rather than later?

CHAPTER TWELVE

ONE MORE GOAL

—PAUL HENDERSON

This is the true joy of life, the being used up
for a purpose recognized by yourself as a mighty one.

GEORGE BERNARD SHAW

A flick of a hockey stick made Paul Henderson a hero on September 28, 1972. It was the 1972 Canada-Russia Summit Series, and Henderson's goal has been called a defining moment for Canadian pride. It's still referred to as the "Goal of the Century."

After eighteen successful years of professional hockey with various teams in the National Hockey League and World Hockey Association, Paul's life took on a new and somewhat unexpected focus. For the next twenty-six years, he would become a Christian leadership mentor to hundreds of men around the world. Paul believes his ministry eclipses the fame of that Canada-Russia hockey series, and his hockey career in general.

Regardless of your particular faith beliefs, the commitment and dedication with which Paul has lived his entire adult life is remarkable. Your faith might not be Christianity, or you might not find faith in organized religion, but don't miss the overarching message: dedication and commitment to something deep inside each of us is larger than human comprehension.

In November 2009, Paul's life took another unexpected turn when he was diagnosed with chronic lymphocytic leukemia. Paul tells us he doesn't have any angst or fear whatsoever. We were referred to Paul by Bruce Etherington.

In his own words, here's how Paul arrived at his incredible sense of peace.

• • • •

I think there are a lot of things you can learn from hockey. You understand the value of working hard, that there aren't any shortcuts, especially to the NHL. No one makes it by accident. In fact, there were a lot of players who were better than I was who didn't make it to the NHL. You learn that you have to really want something badly. If you're not passionate about it, you're not going to get there.

So, to make a difference in anything, you really have to be passionate about it. You have to love to do it. I think that everyone has a sweet spot in life. Everyone is good at something. It's that sweet spot that I've been trying to help people find for the last twenty-six years after going into the ministry. I think I learned from hockey how to find that sweet spot. I loved playing hockey.

I grew up in the little village of Lucknow, Ontario, and, basically, we were poor people. I never had a pair of skates until I was nine. We didn't have many clothes. We had an old car. But I have found that growing up poor was both a curse and a blessing. I became self-sufficient by the time I was fourteen because I knew that my parents were not going to be able to help me. They were not going to help educate me. There wasn't much money for many things, so I learned to work hard and save. I didn't get into drinking or smoking, because that cost money. I was really earning my way so, when I look back, I was fortunate to grow up poor. It helped me to realize at a young age what was important. I realized that you don't have to have a lot to be happy or to feel fulfilled.

When I look back at my father, I remember him as a good man. He worked for the railway and had a wife and five kids. I used to watch him and see that he didn't have any passion for his job, even though it was pretty good pay. And I would look at him and think, I'm never going to do that. I will never, ever do something that I can't get up and be happy about, that I don't want to go to work for. I remember thinking when I was fifteen or sixteen that I was not going to just have an existence.

Fortunately, I had a burning desire to be an NHL hockey player. I would never have made it without that passion. I worked very hard at making it into the NHL because I carved out the time to make it happen. I think that people who have a passion for something are pretty good at it, and they don't mind sacrificing. I was also lucky that I didn't get any really bad injuries, like taking out a knee or shoulder in junior hockey. When I wanted something, I paid the price to get it done. I don't know if these things are ingrained in a person, or if you develop them as a kid growing up.

Even in the ministry, I've never thought of it as a sacrifice, because it was something I really wanted to do. I could have made much more money if I'd gone on as a motivational speaker and given up the ministry, but I knew that was not who I really was. I knew that I had found my niche, my sweet spot.

Hal and Dana introduced me to the concept of *Lifeworth*. For me, the turning point in finding my own definition of *Lifeworth* was when I became a Christian. I knew there was a hole in me and I just couldn't put my finger on why. I started looking into spirituality when I was thirty. It was right after the spring of 1973, when I was still playing professional hockey. I had everything I'd ever dreamed of. I had a great marriage, I was doing something I loved to do, and I was making great money. But I was also filled with anger, frustration, and bitterness. Some anger from the past concerning my relationship with my dad, and some anger during my hockey career, like issues with Harold Ballard, the owner then of the Toronto Maple Leafs. I was ticked off half the time and frustrated with a lot of things.

Then a man, Mel Stevens, came along and asked me, "Paul, have you ever considered the spiritual dimension of life? You've taken care of yourself physically and mentally. You've done well financially. But have you ever given any thought to the spiritual side of life?"

That question really struck a chord because, without knowing it, I hadn't considered that part of my life. About that time, my oldest daughter started to ask me questions about God. I couldn't give her an intelligent, coherent answer. It made me stop and think. I had never slowed down long enough to think about it. I wasn't sure if there was a God.

I became a Christian, by becoming a follower of Jesus, in the spring of 1975. I was really fortunate because two and a half years later I found a wonderful mentor. John Bradford, a very successful businessman, took me under his wing. We met once a week for one and a half hours over three years. This profoundly changed my whole manner of living. He helped me develop a very deep spiritual side to my life. I was very blessed to have had this opportunity to develop this dimension. It changed my life so much for the better in terms of being a better husband, father, friend, and even a hockey player.

After three years participating in this group, Bradford, my mentor and pastor, came to me and said, "Paul, you could truly impact people's lives by becoming a leader and mentor yourself." They really encouraged and pushed me to step out in faith and let God use me to develop other men the way I had been impacted.

At first I didn't want to lead, but they eventually convinced me. I remember thinking, "Man, I haven't been a Christian long enough. I need more training." They had a lot more confidence in me than I had in myself, so they gave me eight guys to work with in a group. I sure was new at it. Pretty green as a leader. But very quickly I could see that the guys were responding to me. I could see that I was changing their lives in the way my mentor had changed mine.

You know, looking back, I thought Christians were a bunch of weak people. I thought, if you can't make it in life, then you had to get God on your side. But I was immature in my thinking. I used to say I was a self-made man. I hadn't had any help from my parents. I went out there, busted my rear end in hockey, and got a few concussions along the way. I was pretty proud of the fact that I had gotten there on my own, but, when I got there, something was missing. When I couldn't answer my kid's questions, I knew there was something missing. And even after I became a Christian, I still didn't fully understand the impact that it would have on my life. I didn't understand everything, but I understood enough to believe that God was who He said He was.

I began to understand that there is a game plan for life for all of us right in the Bible. There is a game plan for being a husband or wife, a father or mother, a friend and a successful business person. It also talks a lot about leaving a legacy after a person is gone. The Bible speaks about what you can do for others, which is really the important thing. We are called to be God's ambassadors. Being part of that group, I saw that the guys were becoming better husbands and starting to have better balance in their lives in terms of what was truly important.

For me, the Bible became my compass, and I know that many people feel uncomfortable talking about things like this. Everyone needs to find his or her own way, regardless of which faith you were raised in or believe in. What I have found is that there are many people just wandering through life without any deep faith at all. What a lonely road. I know; I was on it for a long time.

When I retired from the NHL in 1981, I went to a seminary in the United States for theological training and then came back to Canada in

1984. At that time, I basically felt that I was called to find guys like I used to be, guys who were fairly successful, but thought church was boring and didn't have any interest in spiritual things. My friend, Bruce Etherington, was a guy like that, chasing the almighty dollar but going nowhere, spiritually. I met with him one day and asked him where he was on his spiritual journey. He didn't have a clue what I meant, which started a conversation. I've since had hundreds of those conversations over the years, trying to get guys to realize what's really important in life. I asked them to go to the end of their lives, like going to their funeral and working backwards. I had the guys make a list of the things that were important to them. I knew where they were in their lives because, for thirty-two years, I was there, too. All I was doing was accumulating things and enjoying the good life. I joined the golf club, travelled to nice places, and had the fancy cars. Maybe the good life, but it was all pretty self-centred.

When I first started on my spiritual journey, one of the things my mentor asked me to do was to write a Purpose Statement for myself. It took me nine or ten months. It was two pages long to start with, but, being competitive, I wanted to get it down to a few words. The interesting thing is that, over that period of time, I thought about it, dwelled on it, and rewrote it. Once a person goes through that type of a process, they can really define what they want to do and how they want to do it. If you decide to take the time to write your own Purpose Statement, it will help bring clarity to your life.

So here's mine. It hasn't changed in twenty years. My purpose statement is simply: "To be a Godly world change agent." That's it. That's what motivates me, and it's what I think I've been called to do. As a result, I don't have any desire to retire.

I'm continually asked what does it mean to be "Godly." I would describe that as someone who lives with integrity, someone who would do the things that Jesus would do. I put my complete faith and trust in Jesus each and every day, spending time with Him in prayer, letting Him speak to me from the Bible. This impacts everything I do. "World" means not just being concerned locally, but dreaming of impacting people around the world. Over the last twenty years, I have been to a dozen countries, sharing my spiritual journey with others. "Change agent" simply means changing the direction of people's lives toward deep spirituality found in a relationship with Jesus Christ.

I encourage people to write their own Purpose Statement. But I don't tell them what to write. I just share my experiences and ask questions. A good Purpose Statement is usually one sentence. If you can't get it into one sentence, it's probably not a well-thought-out Purpose Statement.

So flashing ahead, here I am now in my mid-to-late sixties. When I look over my shoulder to my past, I get far more satisfaction from what I've done with my life since hockey than from what I did during hockey. Scoring that goal was a wonderful experience. It was awesome. I was representing my country playing in that series. It was the highlight of my athletic career. But in terms of accomplishments, the last twenty-six years in the ministry makes the peak experience of scoring that historic goal absolutely pale in comparison.

The older I get, the more I realize that a person will always do better being part of a community. The thing about having a deep faith is that you're part of an incredible community. The more you give away, the more that comes back. You try to help other people, but you end up helping yourself. And I think in that community everyone needs a mentor. Man, there is no such thing as a self-made person.

When I was diagnosed with leukemia the first week of November 2009, I can tell you unequivocally that I had no angst whatsoever. I don't have any fear of dying, because I am firmly convinced that this life is not the real game. We're just passing through. It's merely the warm up for eternity, and so I have found the best way to live life down here is to try to help other people. Life is not about always going for the financial gusto and trying to have it all. We are told to provide for our families and to help people around us. When we do, we feel good about it. For me, living with this mindset, I have slowly come to the realization over the years that I'm not as important as I used to think I was. But I know that I can be used by God when I allow Him to lead and guide me, and use the gifts and talents that He has given to me.

Now, fighting cancer, all I can do is get up every day and give it my best shot. And if I wake up tomorrow, I'm going to do the same thing all over again. I'm not going to pull back. I'm not going to withdraw or retire. I've been into this fight with cancer since the latter part of 2009, and I'm going to keep going as best I can. Life is just taking a day, living it to the maximum, and not being fearful about tomorrow. The past is there to learn from and gain wisdom from. The present is where we leave our legacy.

Looking to the future, I have a great desire to improve and be better at everything I do. I have to continually realize that, although I have some strengths, I also have some weaknesses. I would love to be more patient than I am. I would like to be a gentle and humble person. But, in the end, I want to continue to be a significant change agent.

Too many people never slow down enough and take the time to think about their lives, to think about what's important and what's not. I would suggest that after you have read this book take the time to reconnect with yourself. Try to figure out why you are here on Earth and what makes life worth living. This book can really challenge you if you let it. Take the time to craft your personal Purpose Statement.

I suggest that you take care of your soul by developing the spiritual side of life. I wish I had learned that a lot sooner. ■

To learn more about Paul's leadership speaking and training, visit www.leaderimpactgroup.com

SO NOW WHAT?

B eing on purpose means having a dedication and commitment to something deep inside each of us, something that pulls us forward into our future, something we use to guide our decisions as we move forward in our lives. Paul shared and explained his purpose statement: to be a "Godly world change agent." Here are some examples of other purpose statements:

- To enliven, encourage, and re-inspire the love of music for children in public schools.

- To be a mom: to empower independence, self-reliance, and confidence in my children through being a positive role model.

- To be a spokesperson who helps people connect their daily actions to saving the wildlife on our planet.

- To use humour and kindness to help seniors adjust to the changes that come with aging and potential ill health.

- To design and build beautiful wood furniture that brings enjoyment to others.

The challenge to each of us is to take the time to create our own Purpose Statement that describes what we are truly passionate about. We encourage you to explore what your purpose might be at this point in your life. It doesn't have to be long—some of the most effective purpose statements are clear, simple, and related to where you are at this point in your life.

- Is there something in your life that you are so passionate about that you would sacrifice a great deal to achieve it?

- What are you willing to sacrifice?

- Is there something you believe in that you think is more important than your existence or is the purpose of your existence? What is it?

CHAPTER THIRTEEN

RIDING THE
ROLLER COASTER

Life is being on the wire;
everything else is just waiting.

KARL WALLENDA, THE FLYING WALLENDAS

I n reality, life is generally not one peak experience after another. Yes, peak experiences can create very different feelings than those we experience in the Comfort Zone. Yes, they can change the flow of our lives. And, yes, they can help us grow and stretch our limits. But, as we mentioned in an earlier chapter, they are generally short in duration, not sustainable for longer time periods. That means that we spend more of our lifetime in our Comfort Zone than in the Lifeworth Zone. This is just the normal flow of life. So, what about the time we spend in the Comfort Zone?

For many of us, getting into our Comfort Zone and maintaining it is a goal in itself, and most often a challenge. Each person's Comfort Zone is unique, defined by the goals and limits they set for themselves. What income do we require to achieve our needs, wants, and goals? What size of house do we want? What type of car? Where do we want to live? How much education do we want? What physical things do we want or need?

Who do we continue to support or help: our children, parents, grandchildren, various family members, others in need? Do we have enough Time, Talent, and Treasure Marbles to achieve and maintain our needs and wants?

We all have a pretty good idea of how life is expected to go. But it doesn't always turn out as we thought it might. Sometimes we end up where we hoped. At other times, we find ourselves in a different place or in different circumstances than we expected. Some people, in their wildest fantasies, never dreamed they would be making as much money or enjoying the "things" (marbles) they do; while others hoped to have been more financially successful by this time in their lives. Some might have found themselves in the right place at the right time with a lucky business deal. Others might have received that unexpected inheritance. Some may have even won the lottery! Some people thought they would find their soul mate on the first go-around, only to be proven wrong, while others were fortunate enough to grab the brass ring right away. Even with all of life's ups and downs, they still see the person they fell in love with way back when. For others, perhaps none of the above has happened—so far.

We often find ourselves in a "more or less" scenario by mid-life. More weight, less skip in our jump. More wrinkles, less sight. More hair in the wrong places, less hair in the right places. More fat, less muscle. More patience, less ability to hear. Fully acknowledging that we go through phases and understanding that passing through them as we age is part of the deal should make the process less stressful and easier to accept. Recognizing that change is part of the formula should make it easier to accept and understand the ups and downs we encounter. At least in theory.

Life has its ebbs and flows. It's not a stagnant pond with green water and moss. Our lives are like the ocean, where the tide comes in and goes out. It never stops, but the size of the waves can vary. Sometimes you'll see ten footers crashing on the beach. At other times, the waves are gently playing with the sand.

The same is true of our lives. We should expect the ebbs and flows, the peaks and valleys of life. We should expect change. As we mentioned in Chapter 10, emotional and psychological changes often occur as we move from our Comfort Zone into a peak experience. Similar changes take place as we experience the everyday peaks and valleys of our lives and as we move from one phase to another through the aging process. However, these changes generally follow a recurring pattern or cycle.

The transition we make when we are moving from one of the valleys back to one of the peaks or when we are re-engaging in our Comfort Zone can be seen as a recurring process throughout our lives. The processes involved in Free Reining and Breaking Through the Wall apply equally well as we move through the different cycles and phases of our lives. The questions that we ask at each phase are similar to the questions that we suggested you ask at each phase when Breaking Through the Wall. The only difference is that instead of trying to create a peak experience, we may be trying to re-engage in our Comfort Zone and in our life where it is at currently. Or we may be in the process of making a transition into a new phase of our lives, for example from our career to retirement, from parent to grandparent. We have illustrated this cycle in Figure 13.1.

Figure 13.1

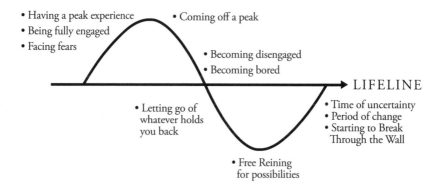

- Having a peak experience
- Being fully engaged
- Facing fears

- Coming off a peak

- Becoming disengaged
- Becoming bored

LIFELINE

- Letting go of whatever holds you back

- Time of uncertainty
- Period of change
- Starting to Break Through the Wall

- Free Reining for possibilities

Imagine being on a roller coaster as it follows a twisting, turning track. As we are racing toward the peak, we are fully engaged in life. We know what we want and why we want it. We're doing what we want to be doing. During this time, we are also successfully facing our fears and challenges.

Inevitably, as we near the top of one of our peaks, we will feel the energy of this phase of our life diminish. We notice that our car seems to be slowing down, clickety-clacketing on the way to the top of the tracks. We may find ourselves slowly becoming disengaged and bored with where we are in life. We start to wonder if this is all there is. You might be asking, "Why am I doing this?"

Then, in one smooth motion, your car moves over the top and heads earthbound. Can you remember that feeling as you crest the peak, hoping the car you are riding in doesn't fall off and crash? Subconsciously, it's the same in life. Just as you reach a peak, you are suddenly plummeting downward and, like a real roller coaster, the "g-force" from that plunge can leave you a bit fearful. This downward plunge may represent the period after a peak experience. We have just experienced the intensity and emotion of that experience and are coming down from that high. It can also represent times when the shine is coming off our Comfort Zone. We feel ourselves becoming less engaged with what we are doing, bored, looking for a change. Maybe we have been at our job too long. Perhaps our children are leaving home and we are wondering what's next. Possibly our marriage is not quite what it used to be. At some point during this phase, we will recognize that we need to make a change. This could simply mean finding ways to become re-engaged and getting back into a positive and rewarding routine. It could also mean that we are searching for some type of peak experience, something to lift us out of the valley we are currently in. It could also mean that we are experiencing a transition in our life, moving from one phase of life into another. We could be entering parenthood for the first time, starting our first (or second) career, moving from being a thirty-something to being a forty-something, or moving from a long career into retirement.

Following the excitement of the plunge, you might find yourself becoming more introspective and reflective. This is a time of letting go, of Free Reining, of re-engineering ourselves, redefining our lives, and setting new priorities and goals. It's the time when a butterfly is getting ready to emerge and spread its colourful wings. As we close in on the valley in the tracks below us, we eventually reach a point where we recognize that change is necessary, that we may be trapped in our Comfort Zone, in a place we don't want to be. As we enter the valley, we recognize the need to start the process of letting go by asking ourselves the same questions that we presented in Chapter 10. What could be holding you back? What is causing the disengagement or boredom? Do you have any fears, anxieties, or trepidations about moving forward to the next phase of your life? What things do you need to keep doing in order to meet your needs?

We also need to start the process of Free Reining to determine what the next phase of our life will be like. Will it take some type of peak experience to help us create a new high in our lives? Do we have to find ways to become re-engaged with our current career? What would you like that phase to look like? What would you definitely not want it to look like? We need to create that clear image of our desired future to help pull us into a new part of our life or into a peak experience.

And, as life goes down, it also goes up. It's as natural and predictable as the sun. We find a way to become re-engaged and start the wild ride up to a new peak in our life. In this phase we gain clarity as to which direction we want our lives to go and we begin to make the necessary changes to head there. We also enter an area of uncertainty, excitement, and challenge as we start speeding upwards. Perhaps it's a change in career, a change or improvement in a marriage, a rededication to faith or fitness, or reorganizing finances and making some tough choices about debt. This is also a time when we begin to face our fears, to take action, and start the process of moving to the next phase. Eventually we will Break Through the Wall. This can be a renewal of where we were in our Comfort Zone, it could be moving into a new phase in our lives, or it could be achieving a peak experience.

This cycle will repeat many times over the course of our lives. It's constant. We never stop going through the phases and cycles as we move along our lifeline. The peaks and valleys of our lives occur as we move through the different phases of the cycle. In Figure 13.2, below, we have illustrated some of the different terms that can describe parts of the cycle over one's life. We put them there to help you see some of the different types of emotions or questions that may arise as you go through different phases. You may recognize a few of the terms or you may even be at one of those points right now.

Figure 13.2

FOCUSED

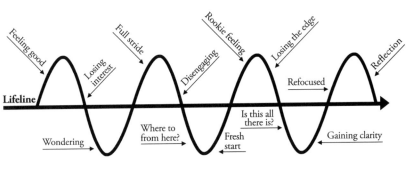

DISENGAGED

Just as with a real-life roller coaster, life is not always just peaks and valleys. We will also have straight stretches, curves left and right, and, heaven forbid, sometimes a complete overhead roll (see Figure 13.3). On the many straight and flat sections, things seem normal and we have a chance to catch our breath (position 1 on Figure 13.3). There may only be the odd small ripple, a small peak or valley. We are back travelling in the upper part of our Comfort Zone, at least until we hit another peak or trough. The length of these comfortable stretches can vary in length, depending on what is happening in our lives. During these times, we generally have enough Time, Talent, and Treasure Marbles to meet most of our needs and many of our wants.

Figure 13.3

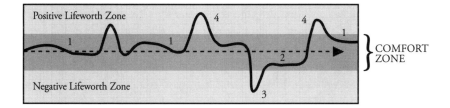

There is another type of flat zone on the tracks that is a bit different than the flat stretches in the upper part of the Comfort Zone (position 2 on the diagram). Sometimes, the tracks take us into a lower zone that is not a drop-off trough. Instead, they gently slope to a lower level and travel along a straight stretch for a while in the lower part of our Comfort Zone. This can be a time of boredom, dissatisfaction, disengagement, sadness, or depression. It can happen to all of us, and for many different reasons. This type of flat stretch can result from an unfortunate experience or negative peak experience (position 3), or from being disengaged or out of focus for too long. It can result from the loss of a job, a concern with personal or business finances, a serious illness or injury, the death of someone close, a divorce, or any number of reasons. There are two key points to remember about these lower-lying flat zones. First, this type of flat stretch can happen to anyone at any time. No one is immune. Second, we can generally choose to move higher into our Comfort Zone (re-engagement) or into a positive peak experience (position 4).

Straight zones on the tracks serve a purpose in our lives. They can provide us with opportunities to reflect on our lives, to review our core values, to focus more on what we feel is our core purpose in life, to plan for change or the next phase of our lives, to plan a peak experience. They are periods of realignment and renewal. Some will turn to their faith for answers and direction. Others may turn to a friend or colleague for an ear or a shoulder. Many may turn to a course or a book for inspiration, looking for some insight and information into human behaviour, perhaps reading stories of others who have travelled through these straight stretches. By looking at ways to reinvent themselves through the lenses of others, most will conquer their boredom, meet their need for change, or deal with sadness, depression, or darkness in their lives. Before they know it, they're back on the race to the next peak in life, shooting back up through their lifeline to find themselves fully engaged and going for it again.

Each of us has our own car on the ride and the roller coaster ride itself is unique to each of us. The tracks themselves are our pathway through life, our lifeline, as we gradually age, always moving forward, never once stopping, and never going back the other way. The roller coaster can't stop its journey until it reaches the end of the line.

Just like the analogy of waves on the ocean, sometimes we find ourselves on a thirty-foot crest and, at other times, it seems we are sailing on glass. The peaks, valleys, curves, and flats can change in height or length over one's life. Just as in nature, there are forces in our lives that may influence our path in life. There are many voices that we may listen to throughout our lives (see Figure 13.4). In our early adult years, our parents and society might influence our decisions and our path in life: "You should go to school and get educated. You should decide on what you're going to do with your life, your career, where you will live. You should get married and have kids, get a mortgage in the suburbs, get a rusted-out minivan and a barking dog."

Figure. 13.4

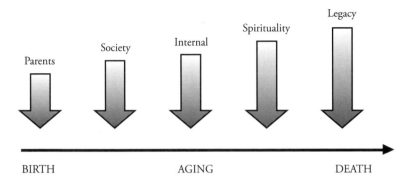

VOICES IN OUR LIVES OVER TIME

In our earlier years, we may have been marching more to society's expectations about what we should be doing with our lives. Decisions have been influenced largely by our perception of what we felt others expected of us. As we age, we slowly start to listen to the voice inside us, a voice that has been there all along, but often ignored. We start to make decisions for ourselves. Some of our decisions might cause others to scratch their heads, wondering what happened to us. But as Dick Lieder comments in his book, *Repacking Your Bags*, this is not a midlife crisis but probably a midlife "inventure." As we approach the midlife years, many of us will start to wonder what we really want out of life, what excites us, what impact we are making in the lives of others. This truly is a time of renewal.

There are also fears and regrets in our lives and, like the moon's gravitational influence on the tides, they can influence our moods and decisions at various points in our life (see Figure 13.5). We wonder what direction our life should take. Will we be able to support ourselves and pay our bills? Will we have enough to meet our core needs? The scarcity mentality is always there, in our subconscious. If we have been fortunate to have enough, when will this bubble burst?

Figure. 13.5

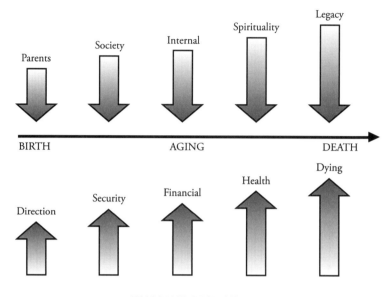

VOICES IN OUR LIVES OVER TIME

FEARS AND REGRETS

As we age, we have the inevitable fears about health and death. "What happens if I get sick? Will I survive cancer if I get it? How long will I live? What legacy will I leave? I wish I had handled my money better. Will anyone know I even existed after I'm gone?"

All of these voices, fears, and regrets influence our ride through life. For some who have lived an even-keeled life and been fairly grounded, the waves have been quite manageable. Others may have had a truly wild roller coaster ride throughout their lives thus far, perhaps through no fault of their own. Their environment may have left them clinging onto their roller coaster for dear life, feet pushing firmly into the floor, head and back pushed into the back of the seat, and sweating hands white-knuckled on the safety bar.

There's no right or wrong with either extreme. Everyone's ride is different.

Everyone walks their own path in life, but knowing the forces, patterns, and voices that influence our life decisions can help us make more sense of the roller coaster ride. Knowing that life is full of ebbs and flows will help each of us understand that change is inevitable. We should welcome and embrace change, understanding that, regardless of which phase we are in, life brings us the opportunity to reinvent ourselves, to step back, refocus, and redefine our priorities and goals. Roller coasters are fun, whether we are at the amusement park or just living life. Throw your hands up in the air, smile, and enjoy the ride, wherever it takes you. ∎

SO NOW WHAT?

We have introduced the different phases that can occur and reoccur throughout your life. We have also suggested that various voices, fears, and regrets influence us. The keys are, first, understanding that the process is normal; second, identifying which phase you might be in; and third, deciding what action you might need to take. It might mean re-engaging yourself in your Comfort Zone, looking at your situation in a different way, reframing it to focus on the positives. It might mean making the transition from one phase of your life to another, starting a new career, becoming a parent for the first time, crossing that once far-off age of fifty, or becoming an empty-nester. It might take a peak experience to help you make these shifts.

Here are some thoughts and questions for you to think about.

* What part of the roller coaster ride or phase are you in right now? Are you in your Comfort Zone and feeling good?

- Are you feeling a bit trapped in your Comfort Zone? Are you looking for change? Is it time to Free Rein out of your Comfort Zone by planning your next peak experience?

- Have you recently experienced an emotionally negative experience that has created a temporary valley or low, flat spot in your life? How are you planning to reclaim control of your life?

- What are the pressures, voices, fears, or regrets at this time in your life? Which ones can you influence or change? Which ones cannot be changed or influenced by you? How will you respond to them?

CHAPTER FOURTEEN

CLIMBING BACK

—ALAN HOBSON

Success is not final, failure is not fatal:
it is the courage to continue that counts.

WINSTON CHURCHILL

As a boy, Alan Hobson dreamed of climbing Mount Everest after seeing pictures of it in books. There was something alluring and magnetic about Everest for him, because, at 8,852 metres (29,035 ft.), it is the world's tallest peak. Although it has claimed the lives of hundreds of climbers, to many other climbers and millions of would-be adventurers worldwide, it is seen as the ultimate physical challenge on Earth. But, as it turned out, Everest was not to be Alan's toughest climb.

It took Alan and his teams three separate attempts and more than a decade of fundraising, training, and organizing to reach the top of the world and return safely. All of his trips were self-guided, self-organized, and corporately sponsored. To stage each of them, he and his teammates had to raise $250,000 to $500,000 in cash, equipment, and supplies. They gathered four to nine tonnes of gear, and recruited between twelve and twenty international team members for each attempt. Despite this massive financing, logistical, and organizational effort, Alan's first two expeditions did not make it to the top. They were deemed failures by most outside observers, but not by Alan and his teammates. It was on his third attempt, in 1997, that he and long-time friend, Calgarian Jamie Clarke, finally set foot on "the Gable of the Gods" that is the roof of the world—a jet stream-scoured cone of snow about the size of a cafeteria table.

Alan thought climbing Everest would be the biggest challenge he would face in his life. Little did he know he would soon tumble from the top of the world to the bottom. It would be a very long fall, and an even harder and longer climb back.

Now living in Canmore, Alberta, in the majestic Rocky Mountains west of Calgary, Alan has written half a dozen best-selling books and is considered to be one of the best adventure speakers in the world. But, like all lives, his has not been without its challenges. By meeting them head-on, he has gained a unique perspective on what can pull us back from the brink, and what can drive us forward to a brighter and wiser future. Alan was referred to us by Dale Ens. Here is Alan in his own words.

● ● ● ●

Hal and Dana asked me when it was that I started to make the transition from networth—mostly thinking about professional and financial achievement—to *Lifeworth*. I can tell you exactly. It was April 6, 2001.

An unforgettable personal journey got me to that point. During the first months of 2000, I had noticed a slow but steady decline in my level of fitness with no change in my daily fitness regime. When I am in peak condition my resting heart rate is usually about fifty to fifty-five beats a minute (seventy to eighty-five is considered normal for a sedentary individual). That's not a very low resting heart rate for a high-performance athlete but that's how my physiology works. Well, before I had taken a single pedal stroke on a stationary bike my heart rate was 110. I wondered what the heck was going on. I'd been feeling tired and run down for months. I had a sore throat, swollen glands, and an upper respiratory infection I couldn't seem to kick. But the real clincher came when I realized that I couldn't swim a length of a twenty-five-metre pool without being totally gassed. I could usually swim for an hour non-stop with ease.

Because I was feeling drained, I went to see my family physician. She took a quick look at me and said, "Oh, you have post-nasal drip. You just need some antibiotics." I took those for about ten days and then I made another appointment to see her. When I got there, I said, "I have good news and bad news. The good news is that my sore throat's gone. Thank you so much! The bad news is I have something way more serious than post-nasal drip. Please get me a blood test."

That was a Monday. I got the results of the blood test on Tuesday. By Wednesday I had been referred to a blood specialist and on Friday he told me that I had acute leukemia—an aggressive cancer of the blood. Ninety percent of the cells in my bone marrow were cancerous. Without treatment, he said that I had less than a year to live. Even with treatment, there was an 85 percent chance I would die. He considered that my condition was so serious that he wanted to admit me into the hospital to begin my first week of round-the-clock chemotherapy that night. I wasn't going to get the chance to go home and pack. I wasn't even going to have time to go to the cafeteria for a sandwich. I was going straight to the acute-care cancer ward—*now!*

As I'm sure you can imagine, this news hit me hard. I felt like my world had been turned upside-down. But despite the gravity of my situation, I simply wasn't mentally prepared for what he was proposing to do next. So, I insisted on taking a few days to shut down my business, let my friends and family know what had happened, and steel myself mentally for the rigours of the inner Everest ahead.

Our bodies have an innate intelligence. They send us signals when something isn't right. In my case, the signs had been there for quite some time, but I'd put them off to business stress and travel-related fatigue and burnout. Nevertheless, I wasn't completely surprised by the diagnosis. I have learned in my life, though, that in a crisis the sooner we move from anxiety to action, especially intelligent action, the stronger our strategic position can become. Action is the greatest antidote to fear. So, together with my personal and professional caregivers, we quickly developed a treatment plan. In an exceptional gesture of loyalty, love, and commitment, my best friend and financial planner, Dale Ens, stepped up to the plate to offer to handle all my financial affairs.

"I only want you to focus on one thing—getting better," he counselled. "For the next six months, that's where I want you to put your entire focus. I'll take care of the rest." I share that powerful experience with Dale in my book *Climb Back from Cancer*.

Over the next four months, I went through three rounds of week-long, 24/7 chemotherapy as an in-patient—over five hundred hours—to put my leukemia into remission. That included 128 hours of high-dose chemotherapy to completely eliminate my immune system. Then, on November 15, 2000, I had an adult blood stem cell transplant, the modern-day equivalent of a bone marrow transplant. My donor was my second-eldest brother, Eric. Curiously, I did not match with my own fraternal twin, James.

I am so unbelievably fortunate. My transplant has been a huge success story for this kind of cancer, which has a survival rate of 15 percent or less in the first year. My climb back has been beyond my wildest dreams, because I am as physically fit as I was before my last Everest expedition in 1997. I have made a 100 percent recovery, have been cancer-free for over ten years, and am now considered officially medically cured. Physically, other than a little grey hair and a few more wrinkles, I look pretty much the same on the outside. After chemotherapy, I'm thankful to have any hair at all!

Inside, however, I am significantly different. As a result of the transplant, I now have two types of DNA in me. The DNA in my organs is my own, but the DNA in my blood is my brother's. I am a genetically modified human! Eric and I are, quite literally, blood brothers. It's a magical and profound reality.

Some people lament the passing of the years. I actually celebrate them because, for me, every day is not only a gift, it's a bonus. I am not only living on borrowed time loaned to me by God, medical science, a superb healthcare system, my then-fiancée, and incredibly supportive family and friends, but I am spending this inner inheritance with a sense of fervent urgency. Tomorrow is not a given. I believe that we shouldn't just seize the day; we should ingest it, digest it, and use it as fuel to fire our future—if we're fortunate enough to have one. Every moment is precious and priceless. That's not to say I don't have moments of frustration, fear, self-doubt, anxiety, and anger. We all do as human beings. But when those moments occur, I try to remind myself that there is privilege even in pain. At least I am alive to experience emotions.

My recovery from cancer has proven to be many times harder than climbing Everest. When I came out of treatment and transplant, my biggest challenge was being able to stand in the shower long enough to wash. I timed it. It was fifty-three seconds. I could not stand for more than fifty-three seconds. It was more than frightening; it was terrifying. Everest and the inner Everest of cancer have given me a whole new perspective on life, death, tenacity, and triumph. They've also given me a chance to reconsider how we approach some of our biggest life challenges.

We use words like "beat," "defeat," "assault," and "conquer" when we talk about the challenge of cancer in much the same way we use them when we talk about climbing Everest. We take a combative approach to cancer (and many other diseases and ailments) and we put all our focus on fighting the illness, rather than healing from it. That induces an instinctive fight-or-flight response in us that is based in fear. Fear is weaker than courage, just as darkness is weaker than light. Light will penetrate darkness, but darkness cannot penetrate light. We don't so much want to get cancer out of our bodies, as we want to let healing in.

Putting our focus on fighting rather than healing is a bit like focusing on fighting the wind instead of focusing on our feet when we're climbing a mountain. It may give us something on which to concentrate, but it doesn't necessarily get us to where we want to go in the most efficient and effective way possible. In the case of cancer, what we really want to do is overcome. We not only want to survive the disease, if we can we want to thrive beyond it. We don't just want to fight; we want to prevail. That means that we must use our most vital resource—our energy—as if it were life itself, because it *is* life itself.

If you or someone you know is "fighting" or "battling" cancer and that strategy is working for them, that's great. They should stick with it. I personally favour flowing around obstacles rather than fighting them. So, every time a fresh bag of chemotherapy was put up on my I.V. pole, I did not see it as a bag of noxious chemicals that would burn its way through my system. I saw it as a bag of clear white grape juice that would smoothly flow into my body, do its work as powerful medicine and smoothly flow out. This mindset, coupled with anti-nausea medications, meant that I had very few adverse reactions to chemotherapy.

We can no more conquer cancer than we can conquer Everest. If we're lucky, we survive it. And if we are fortunate enough to survive and emerge with most of our faculties intact, we can learn from our experience. We can make significant physical, philosophical, psychological, emotional, and spiritual life changes that can be invaluable to us. When it comes to cancer or any other life-threatening condition, if we survive, change isn't optional; it's essential.

Just as I was frightened by cancer, I was also frightened by Everest. Who wouldn't be? At more than five and a half miles (8,800 metres) above sea level, its summit is the only place on the planet where the jet stream winds actually touch the surface of the Earth. And they don't just touch it, they tear at it—with sometimes greater-than-hurricane-force winds of up to 175 miles per hour (about 280 km/h). The mountain stands head and shoulders above its nearest neighbours and in so doing makes a silent statement of pre-eminence that is undeniable. It has a presence and a power. I still physically shake when I look up at its staggering immensity. *Chomolungma*, the Tibetan word for Everest meaning "Mother Goddess of the World," has a long and storied history filled with epic tales of trial, tragedy, and triumph. That is what lured me to the mountain as a boy. I wanted to know how anyone could survive for weeks there with insufficient sleep, food, oxygen, and only minimal shelter in one of the harshest and most dangerous environments on Earth. "What was it?" I wondered. I wanted to find out.

My first two expeditions to Everest (after seven previous expeditions to other high altitude peaks worldwide) were universally regarded as "failures" by the outside world. We didn't make it to the top on either of them. After seven years of preparation, our first expedition missed the summit by 3,000 vertical feet (915 metres) when our high camp was blasted off the mountain by near-hurricane force winds. Our second expedition missed the summit by an excruciatingly disappointing two city blocks. Our lead climber developed life-threatening high altitude sickness and we chose to try to rescue him rather than continue blindly for the goal. The effort took us thirty-three continuous hours, and it was one of the hardest physical things I had done before climbing back from cancer. I tell the gripping story of that expedition in my book, *From Everest to Enlightenment*. We only fail when we fail to learn from our experiences. So, after each expedition we made a list of all the things that we had learned and what we would do differently the next time. By the time the third expedition came around in 1997, we simply made fewer mistakes until we eventually put the key in the metaphorical lock at the top of the world and miraculously, the door to the summit opened. With permission from the mountain and by the grace of God, we stepped across the threshold briefly and took a few unremarkable photographs in the bitter cold and rarefied air. Then we descended as "quickly" as we could, safely back down to our high camp. All our expedition members reunited in base camp a few days later with all of our fingers, toes, and relationships intact. It was a true team triumph.

What defines us as human beings is not what we do when things go as hoped, it's how well we bounce back from setbacks and how we react to and learn from our "failures." If there is a summit door to success in life, that is one of the master keys. The key to success is failure—how we frame our "failures" and how we realize their networth when all the disappointment is removed. That is a theme consistent throughout history. Martin Luther King Jr., Nelson Mandela, Mohandas Gandhi, Mother Teresa, Antarctic explorer Ernest Shackleton, and Sir Edmund Hillary all overcame incredible odds, obstacles, and setbacks on the path to the realization of their goals and dreams.

Which takes us back to that fateful day of April 6, 2001, when I began to make the transition from networth to *Lifeworth*, as Hal and Dana have so aptly coined it. Four months after my adult blood stem cell transplant, I was invited to be a last-minute substitute speaker at a major cancer centre fundraising luncheon in Newport Beach, California. I was still weak from the transplant and I wasn't even sure if I was physically or psychologically ready to return to the stage. The scheduled speaker, Dr. Jerri Nielsen—who had diagnosed herself with breast cancer while working at the South Pole—had been unable to make it to the event so I had been asked to stand in for her on short notice.

This was to be only my second presentation since coming out of the hospital, and my first cancer audience. When I stepped to the stage, hundreds of patients, survivors, caregivers, healthcare professionals, donors, and community leaders were in the room. I thought of what courage, compassion, and commitment they represented. Thanks in part to them and the thousands of others pushing cancer care forward in the U.S. and Canada, I was out of the hospital, back on my feet and back speaking. It was a powerful realization. Slowly, I began my presentation. I blended my Everest experiences with my cancer ones and, at the end of my program, the audience rose to their feet, and applauded our collective triumph. I was so grateful just to be there.

As I wrote in *Climb Back from Cancer*, at that moment I had an epiphany. Until then I had believed that I had been born to climb Everest so that I could positively affect others by talking and writing about it. Now I realized I had climbed Everest so that I could survive cancer and help others survive and thrive beyond it. The next step in my life's journey had now been revealed. Suddenly, my perspective shifted from "being" a survivor to "knowing"—and knowing in my being what it was I had to do. I had to inspire others to climb back. I had to empower them to overcome their own obstacles, scale their own summits, and remember that we are all pilgrims put here for a purpose.

At last I knew my life purpose. It was not to climb Everest. Everything that I had been doing to that point in my life had been preparing me for this new adventure. I was being groomed for a different role. This realization poured over me like a cleansing shower. It was both affirming and electrifying. For the first time, I understood my illness. As I began to hug and shake hands with the audience members, I realized that it wasn't about me. It was about *we*—the two out of every three people who are diagnosed with cancer who now survive the disease. At this time, we number about twelve million in North America, and our ranks increase by about a million every year. The number of cancer survivors is exploding!

I now knew that I had to get completely healthy. I had to get my life back if I was to begin to try to fulfill this new purpose. So, three times a week I followed a program of mild, individualized cardiovascular activity developed by a crackerjack team of exercise physiologists at the University of Calgary. It consisted of thirty minutes of mild cardiovascular activity (e.g., hiking, biking, walking, jogging, swimming, etc.) on the first day, fifteen minutes of more intense cardiovascular activity two days later, and twenty minutes of moderate aerobic activity two days after that. Within weeks, my energy increased significantly and eventually returned to what it had been before my illness. This led to a groundbreaking medical study from which has evolved the Climb Back from Cancer Program.

My theory, as yet unproven, is that invasive treatments like chemotherapy and radiation significantly weaken the body's oxygen (i.e., energy) delivery systems. The capillaries, those tiny blood vessels where the exchange of oxygen takes place between the bloodstream and the tissues, are likely substantially damaged during treatment. In the process, we can become like hypoxic high altitude climbers; we're not getting enough oxygen. But if we *gently* stimulate the capillaries to rebuild with *mild, individualized cardiovascular activity*, they can.

The challenge for cancer survivors is that we seem to fall into one of three camps. The members of the first camp believe that our energy will come back on its own. The members of the second camp believe that we're too tired to try (or to continue). And the third—the one of which I was a member—holds that if we just try hard enough and long enough, we'll eventually succeed. All three camps need to come together to form a new expedition with a fresh perspective, because all three beliefs are actually misconceptions. In my case, trying too hard only increased my fatigue and weakness. Because of my deep-seated belief in the adage of "no pain, no gain," I could not get my energy level back to where it had been before treatment. But with mild, individualized cardiovascular activity three times a week, I was able to re-energize my body and restart my life. Less very definitely can be more.

Now that I have returned to full health and fitness more than ten years later, I am continuing to try to fulfill my life purpose. When we are living on task and on purpose, everything is clearer. We succeed on purpose. The challenge is that sometimes we either don't know how to find our purpose, or we find it and then lose it. Then we struggle—sometimes for years—trying to find it again. The surest way to find our life purpose is to follow our heart. The surest way to lose it is to lead with our head.

It's easy to lose touch with our purpose. Today's technological capabilities and devices give us ample opportunity for distraction. In fact, we live in the age of distraction. We've "got" to have the latest piece of technology or, as my friend Dale Ens once put it: "the latest solution to a problem we don't have." We're running hard, trying to get more done in less time, make more money, or accumulate more stuff. More, more, more. Faster, faster, faster. We just keep running because we've now been doing it for so long that it's become second nature. Multitasking is mainstream. It's expected. In the age of distraction we are rarely 100 percent present with anything or anyone, sometimes even with ourselves. The moment we stop running against the technological clock, we fear we could fall behind and never catch up. The electronic avalanche of information (what I call the "e-valanche") will bury us—alive, but dead to our true potential and purpose. There is a difference between activity and productivity. One gets us through the day. The other can get us to our dreams. As Gandhi once said, "There is more to life than increasing its speed."

Paradoxically, I believe that one of the keys to speed is stillness. If we make time to be still—if we force ourselves to slow down—our whole perspective on life can change. Like the sediments in a swiftly moving river that gradually slows down, all the distractions in our lives can gradually settle out. Our internal waters can become still and our way forward can become clearer. What we're left with is the vision, peace, and clarity that come from seeing what's truly important in our lives. All this because we took the time—we *made* the time—to slow down. That is what cancer forced me to do; it forced me to slow down. In fact, it brought my life to a screeching halt, at least temporarily. Before cancer, I travelled two hundred or more days a year as a speaker and author. I didn't have a life, a life partner, a home, many outside interests, or even many friends. My life was my business and my business was my life on the road: planes, trains and automobiles, hotels and restaurants, but gratefully, fitness centres. It was a busy and privileged life, for which I am immeasurably grateful, but it was often empty. It was always lonely. It is possible to have a high standard of living but a low quality of life.

Life for me now is very different. Thanks to cancer, I cut my number of speaking presentations in half and with it, my travel. I moved to the mountains, purchased a home, got married, and bought a dog. Sadly, through a parting of the ways, I lost both a fabulous wife and a wonderful dog, but I am a better person and will be a better partner because of it. I still enjoy an exceptionally high quality of life, literally. I spend as much time above the tree line as possible. Where I live, that's the alpine area at least 7,500 feet (2,285 metres) above sea level, where the growing season is so short and the soil so thin that no trees can survive. It is there that I gain a priceless perspective on life. In the valley below, I can get lost in what I'm convinced is "important" and I sometimes can't see the forest for the trees. But up there, I can see the forest *and* the trees. I reconnect with the rhythms of nature, the majesty of the mountains, and the energy of Earth. In doing so, I reconnect with myself and a deep inner peace.

When I return to civilization below, I try to bring that peace into my daily life. Through my speaking, presentations, books, and other initiatives, I endeavour to bring light into the lives of others. Like everyone's evolution, my life is a work in progress, but I am very definitely making progress. Were it not for cancer, I might still have more air miles than smiles and be spending more time in hotels than at home. That's the difference between networth and *Lifeworth*. Networth is about money. *Lifeworth* is about meaning. We may calculate networth by subtracting our debts from our assets, but we achieve *Lifeworth* when we add quality to our lives and to the lives of others. That's a journey worth taking and a climb worth making. In my tumble from the top of the world to the bottom, I have climbed back to the realization that success isn't about height; it's about depth. ■

For more information on Alan's books, speaking presentations, and the Climb Back from Cancer Program, visit www.climbback.com

---

SO NOW WHAT?

Alan's story provides us with great examples of how failure can be a tool to achieving future success. He encourages us to reframe our "failures" and recognize their value, once we get over the initial disappointment. He also emphasizes the importance of taking time to reflect on our lives, to be still for a moment, to reconnect with who we are. The purpose of this reflection is to help us identify or reconnect with what we believe our purpose is in life, what is truly important to us.

• Have you had any setbacks or failures in achieving a peak experience or goal in your past? How did you handle them? What did you learn from them? How can you build on that knowledge?

- When was the last time you actually slowed down enough to reflect on what you are doing with your life? Can you take a one- or two-day break to focus on your life at this point? Can you block out some time each week, maybe an early morning coffee or early evening walk, to think about where you would like to go with your life?

- What words would you use to describe the current quality of your life? Are they the words you would like to be using? If not, which words would better describe the quality of life you desire?

- What changes do you have to make so that you can describe your quality of life the way you want to?

CHAPTER FIFTEEN

FINISHING
STRONG

When it's over, I don't want to wonder if I have made of my
life something particular and real ...
I don't want to end up simply having visited this world.

MARY OLIVER, AMERICAN POET

A t different times in our lives, all of us wonder about our life expectancy. We think about our family's longevity. How long did our grandparents live? Maybe they are still living. Are life-threatening diseases such as cancer or heart disease prevalent in our family's medical history? It's not a "dark" or morbid thing to wonder about. Dying is predictable. The last time anyone checked, the dying ratio was still one to one.

But discussing death can be uncomfortable. Some people are so uncomfortable with the topic that they dismiss it. "Who cares? Why do we need to talk about that? That's just outright depressing." From time to time, consciously or subconsciously, we all wonder or worry about dying. If you haven't, you are now. In Chapter 7, we introduced you to the concept of bits in your mouth that might hold you back. The fear of dying can be one of those bits, and, as we age, the fear increases and so does the pull-back pressure on the bit. We feel that time is running out. This can be one of the most difficult bits to let go. Yet we must, if we are to truly comprehend this terminal reality and to live our lives with a heightened sense of comfort and freedom.

As a society, we do what we can to stop or slow the aging process. We exercise and diet, we have regular check-ups, and we spend millions on vitamins and supplements. Some get hair transplants, Botox injections, face lifts, or chin and tummy tucks. But that doesn't change the inevitable. Human beings were designed to age. We are not designed to last forever. We think that auto makers and technology manufacturers are the kings at planned obsolescence, designing their products with an estimated shelf life and with scheduled updates, new models, upgrades, recalls, repairs, and maintenance along the way. But there isn't a manufacturing company out there that can match the planned obsolescence built into the human body. We have been created to wear out, deteriorate, and gradually fall gently toward the Earth. We are supposed to slow down, get wrinkled, and have our sight and hearing fade away. We are expected to stop functioning some day. Some day the engine won't start. It's right in the owner's manual.

Not knowing the day and time that we will die can feel like travelling on a moving sidewalk in a large international airport. These sidewalks are the craziest things. Starting in the middle of nowhere, seeming to go nowhere, just straight-ahead-Fred, and then dumping you off in a heap at the end, still in the middle of nowhere. And just as in life, we can't get off when we feel like it. We have to wait until the end, even if we are passing our gate. Amazing! And these moving sidewalks are comfortable, aren't they? Letting us just stand there, letting things just happen. Gate after gate, comfortable, no energy exerted, just hanging out in a kind of temporary Comfort Zone. And then it happens. Not paying attention, looking around, looking back, and *bam!*—we get dumped off at the end of the walkway. Now that's really embarrassing, isn't it? Just about twisting an ankle, bags flying all over, desperately trying not to fall flat on our face and, in the end, attempting to make it look as if we intended the whole thing to happen, that tell-tale little jog everyone does that trumpets to the world: "Everything's cool. I saw it coming. Really, I did."

In a real life Comfort Zone, we can find ourselves just standing and watching life go by, gate after gate, month after month, year after year. Like the moving sidewalk, life is dropping us off at the other end. We don't know where or when it will end and dump us. This is the crux of one of life's overarching fears, one of the biggest "bits" in our mind, this fear of the unknown. It applies to many different parts of our lives, but most strongly to our inevitable death. The fear of death can handcuff us. And, for the most part, the handcuffs get tighter and tighter as more Time Marbles leave our bag.

Now let's put the moving sidewalk into total darkness, and with us not knowing if it will simply disappear. Can you imagine being on a moving sidewalk in an airport, but in total darkness? Just think of how you would be wondering and waiting for the sidewalk to end and, there you go again, stumbling and bumbling, trying not to slam your face into the carpet. It's not knowing when our moving sidewalk will disappear that can keep us from taking some of the necessary risks to move out of our Comfort Zone.

Life's moving sidewalk is dumping people off at the other end with calculated consistency. Approximately 250,000 Canadians step off their sidewalks into eternity every year. That's about one every two minutes. By the time you read this chapter, a number of people will have reached the end of their moving sidewalks, some sooner than they expected and some later than they might have thought.

We know we will die some day, but not knowing when, we feel (or hope) it's far away. "Dying young won't happen to me; that's for someone else." But even if we think of it as far away, the fear is there, deep down in a place we seldom visit: the fear of leaving this life, leaving our families and friends, our bag of marbles, leaving things unaccomplished. The fear that we will not have made a difference, left our imprint in life, or be remembered. The fear of dying is as old as the human race. Chuang-Tzu (369–286 B.C.) wrote: "The birth of man is the birth of his sorrow. The longer he lives, the more his anxiety to avoid unavoidable death. What bitterness. He lives for what is always out of reach. His thirst for survival in the future makes him incapable of living in the present."

Many of us have had experiences with people who knew their time was up. They could see the end of their moving sidewalk but did not know what lay beyond. However, they still had time to wrap up their affairs and to say goodbye. What a gift that was for them. What a gift that was for their families and friends. Knowing the end is coming can certainly be a gift. Nick (not his real name) knew that. He was thirty-two when Hal first met him. Here is Hal's powerful experience with Nick in Hal's own words.

I had been in the Rocky Mountains riding horses with a few friends for a couple of days. It was an annual get-together with guys who knew how to ride and what to expect when riding deep into the mountains. At the end of the day, we would gather back at camp, start a bonfire, have a few "pops," tell jokes, and laugh about the day on horseback.

The next day, I needed to be up at dawn to help put on a Stampede breakfast at our local hospice. I sit on the board of the Foothills Country Hospice built by our community at a cost of $4.5 million, all of which was completed with donations, fundraisers, and grants.

Our hospice helps approximately one hundred souls

per year with their final journey on Earth. It's a fabulous facility and sits in the foothills, with a terrific view of the Rockies. Each room has a bed for the patient, another for a family member, and a private bathroom.

We were putting on the pancake breakfast to mark the opening day of the Calgary Stampede. We had griddles, country music, bales of hay to sit on, and lots of friendly laughter. The volunteer board members were hosting the breakfast for the benefit of the staff, families, and those patients who were able to come out. One of my jobs was to load bales of hay at the barn and bring them out to the hospice.

It was a beautiful summer day, the sun just coming up as I arrived at the barn to throw the bales into my horse trailer. I was tired from the last few days riding in the mountains, from the late nights around the fire, and I had a slight headache. I was not in a great mood to volunteer that morning. As I grudgingly tossed sixty-pound hay bales into the trailer, I wondered, "Why am I doing this? How do I get roped into these things?" The conversation I was having with myself was truly pathetic. Poor me. So self-centred.

I eventually arrived at the hospice, trailer full of hay in tow. I rolled up to the large circular driveway in the front to check in. That's when I first met Nick. He was sitting in sweatpants on the front porch, enjoying the summer sunrise. As I walked up to the front door, he greeted me with a warm good morning and said, "Nice horse trailer." I grunted something back as I walked by.

A half hour later, we had the pancake breakfast all set up beside the rose garden: country music playing, griddle cooking away, and folks starting to come out and enjoy the gathering. I saw this same fellow from the front porch carefully walking out, using a walker. He walked slowly, deliberately, and had tubes running from a machine mounted on his walker to his nose. I recognized him from our brief greeting earlier, but I hadn't mentally slowed down enough then to notice the tubes.

He sat down on the bale next to me and again greeted me with "Good morning," but this time extended his hand and said, "I'm Nick." I shook his hand and introduced myself and told him I was a volunteer board member. I hesitated for a minute but then continued, "I have to say you don't seem old enough to be a patient here." He went on to tell me that he was, and that he had been diagnosed with cancer, which had quickly spread to his bones. He had less than three months to live. It's a requirement to be a patient at the hospice that life expectancy is under three months.

I asked how he came to know of our new hospice, which had only opened its doors for patients six months earlier. Nick told me that he had looked at the few hospices in Calgary, only fifteen minutes away, but that none met his needs or they were full at the time. A friend had heard about a new hospice in the country and, through a Google search, Nick found it and applied through the regular medical channels.

Nick told me that when he arrived in the ambulance and the attendants opened the doors, he was speechless when he saw the hospice. He told me as we sat on the hay bales in that warm July summer morning that this was his "gateway to Heaven" and that he "felt lucky to be here."

"You feel lucky?" I asked.

Nick replied, "I've come to terms with the fact that I'm dying. We all are going to die. I just know that it will be soon. I can stay here in my final days, comfortable knowing that my young family can see that I'm in good care."

I sat there blown away with his attitude. There he was, knowing he would die very soon and that he would be leaving his wife and two children, ages eleven years and fourteen months. Earlier, there I was, feeling put out for having to toss some hay around and be part of putting on that breakfast. What an attitude adjustment that was! A real chain yanking. After breakfast, I gladly pitched those heavy hay bales back in the trailer to take back to the barn.

Nick was able to be friends with death. He was able to say his goodbyes. He slipped away about two months later, just as the sun was coming up.

How often do we get caught up in the "me" world, taking the good things in life for granted and wondering why there aren't more. It sometimes takes an experience like this to truly realize that we are just sitting there in our Comfort Zone. Life is precious and should not be taken for granted. Death is normal and not to be feared.

Many of us also fear the death of a loved one: a spouse, a child, a parent or grandparent, a close friend. These people help us meet many of our needs in life, our Existence needs, Relationship needs, or Growth needs. If we lose someone close to us, there is an instant void in our lives. The ability to meet our needs is intertwined with our relationships with these people. Looking at our fear of death from this perspective challenges us to make the most of our relationships with those we love. These can be peak experiences in their own right. We often take these relationships for granted, only to regret doing so once that person is gone.

Why this brief discourse on death? Here's why: the ever-present spectre of dying can be one of the big bits in our mouth that keeps us from moving out of our Comfort Zone. On the flip side, though, we can use this fear to live for today—to Free Rein and dream of possibilities. We can reframe our view of the inevitable and use that energy in a positive way. It can provide us with the most basic of motivations to reach out to achieve as many peak experiences as possible for ourselves, our families, our friends, and for others.

We refer to this alternative view of dying as "Finishing Strong." We can accept the inevitable and get on with the process of living and moving out of our Comfort Zone. This doesn't mean we have to wait until the end of our lives to make one big attempt to break out of the zone. Instead, this can become a way of living the time that we have left in a purposeful way. Remember that we said peak experiences are transitory; they are not sustainable over a longer period of time. That's why they are called peak experiences. We always return to our Comfort Zone, even though it has changed following the peak experience. Once back in the Comfort Zone, we can begin plotting and planning another peak experience. We can even plan multiple peak experiences over time.

John Davidson underwent several peak experiences through Jesse's Journey, pushing his son across Ontario, a record-setting walk across Canada, and eventually the loss of his son. But he has a more distant peak experience that he wants to accomplish, that of raising enough funds for the Jesse

Davidson Endowment to generate $1 million a year for research.

Lindsay Sears has had several peak experiences in her lifetime, including becoming the World Barrel Racing Champion and putting a smile in the hearts of terminally ill Cody Stephens and his family. However, Lindsay continues to seek peak experiences in her life in her quest to win another world championship. She uses her reputation and talent to make a difference in the lives of people she hasn't yet met, especially young girls who want to be barrel racers and look up to her as their role model.

Alan Hobson achieved one of the most physically demanding challenges on Earth by summiting Mount Everest. But his later peak experience, surviving cancer, was an even greater accomplishment. Alan continues to seek out peak experiences every time he speaks about "Climbing Back from Cancer" across North America. He knows that he has provided hope to many individuals as part of this journey.

Peak experiences have become a way of life for the people whose stories appear in this book. The types, intensities, and focuses of those experiences are different for each one, but the trend is undeniably there. We don't know where the desire to have peak experiences comes from. What we do know is that each peak experience is unique to each person. No two people can experience the same peak experience in exactly the same way. We know that peak experiences can be life-changing events, and that they occur outside of our Comfort Zones, in what we call the Lifeworth Zone. We know that they can be planned or unplanned, and can be achieved with the Time, Talent, and Treasure Marbles we have at any given point, or which we can acquire to make the experiences happen. And we know it's important to finish strong, every day, every week, every month, and every year. It's important to deliberately Free Rein to figure out what your next peak experience could be. From there it is necessary to be on-purpose about achieving your peak experience, to make it happen and finish strong within the time frame you have decided on. If you want to take a month to volunteer somewhere in the world, set the goal and do it. Find out what bits or fears are holding you back and then start to let go of the reins, overcome those fears, feel your peak experience pull you into your future, and experience the exhilaration of accomplishing your goal.

Paul Henderson has used his hockey fame to reach out to people as part of his Christian leadership program. Each time Paul begins working with a new group, he creates a peak experience that aligns with his purpose in life at that moment. Do you think Paul thought he would score the Summit Series-winning goal back in 1972? Most likely not. The original peak experience had been to make it onto Team Canada and play in the Canada-Russia series. Scoring three game-winning goals and the series-winning goal happened because of his desire for the original peak experience. We never know what other experiences we will have when we set out on one peak experience.

Katy Hutchison experienced the devastating peak experience of losing her husband through a senseless, needless crime. She subsequently published a book, which was then turned into a movie, both peak experiences. But she hasn't stopped there. She continues to create peak experiences by speaking across Western Canada, delivering her message of forgiveness. Katy didn't expect to be a widow or an author and a speaker after the peak experience of losing her husband. Those peak experiences grew out of the original devastating event.

Jeanelle Mitchell set out to write her first cookbook, *For the Love of Soup,* simply to financially assist her sister and her sister's family. This was a peak experience in itself. However, it turned into a best-selling cookbook and led to the peak experience of writing a second best-seller. Through all of this was the peak experience of being able to help her sister at a time of great need.

Dawn Straka turned her passion for caring for others into many peak experiences starting early in her life as a young volunteer nurse in Africa.

Many years later, in her retirement years, her passion for helping others continues to create experiences through her involvement at the upper leadership levels of Rotary and delivering hundreds of wheelchairs through the same organization to those in need.

Susan Wetmore had no idea that her first volunteer assignment with Canadian Executive Services Overseas would turn into many more trips and assignments around the world. With each trip, she had the opportunity to create another peak experience by helping others learn how to better meet their own needs.

Martha Birkett set out to ride her horse across Canada for the Children's Wish Foundation. She planned that peak experience. The people she met and the lives she touched along the ride became many unplanned peak experiences that grew out of her original plan. During the trip, a small boy gave her a puppy, which she named Chance. Chance finished the ride with Martha and has become a lifelong companion. Martha still marvels at the single marble she received from a young girl who had no money but reached into her marble bag to give Martha her favourite treasure. Martha met many new people who rode along with her for short periods and shared their stories with her.

Tom Droog likely never dreamed as a young man that he would create the Spitz International success story and all the positive peak experiences along the way. Tom also never expected he would lose the love of his life when Emmy passed away shortly after Spitz had been sold. Both were peak experiences, one positive, one negative, but there were opportunities to grow from each, nonetheless. Tom is paying it forward by helping the youth he comes into contact with. A stream of continual peak experiences propels him forward in life to bigger and even more purposeful opportunities.

The interviews we did when writing this book were definitely peak experiences for us. For every person we have profiled here, we are sure you will know someone with similar successes and who faced and overcame similar obstacles in life. As human beings, we can see possibilities and draw strength and inspiration by reading examples of how others are intentionally trying to live their lives on purpose as they have each defined it. Each of us has our own path to follow and our own purpose in life. The overarching theme through all of the stories here was not only the interviewees' commitment to defining their path and their goals, but to having the courage and inner strength to stay the course, to not take their eye off of their goal, to Break Through the Wall, no matter how difficult.

It is tempting to stay in the security and ease of our respective Comfort Zones. Peak experiences will then occur just by happenstance, like an un-planned rainbow. We will all have unplanned peak experiences, good or bad. Living life to the fullest and in a purposeful way requires that we think about our lives, think about the "bits" that may be holding us back, think about what we fear, and take the steps to face those fears head on. That's when life truly gets interesting. That's when we will feel truly alive, engaged, and focused, at least for a while.

Lifeworth is not a one-trick pony, not a one-time event, not a single well-made plan. *Lifeworth* is a new way to live life, but it takes commit-ment and a constant reminder about what's truly important in life. The Time Marbles are flying out of our bags, but don't panic; you're one step closer to finishing strong. You are now aware of what needs to be done— every day. It is up to you to take action.

What are you going to do about it? ∎

BIBLIOGRAPHY

Alderfer, Clayton. *Existence, Relatedness, and Growth: Human Needs in Organizational Settings*. New York: Free Press, 1972.

Bridges, William. *Transitions, Making Sense of Life's Changes*, 2nd Edition. Cambridge: Da Capo Press, 2004.

Bridges, William. *The Way of Transition*: Cambridge: Da Capo Press, 2001.

Carse, James. *Breakfast at the Victory*. San Francisco: Harper, 1995.

Hudson, Frederic M. and Pamela D. McLean. *Life Launch: A Passionate Guide to the Rest of Your Life*, 2nd Edition. Santa Barbara: The Hudson Institute Press, 1996.

Leider, Richard J. *The Power of Purpose: Creating Meaning in Your Life and Work*. San Francisco: Berrett-Koehler Publishers Inc., 2004.

Leider, Richard J. and David A. Shapiro. *Claiming Your Place at the Fire: Living the Second Half of Your Life on Purpose*, 2nd Edition. San Francisco: Berrett-Koehler Publishers Inc., 2004.

Leider, Richard J. and David A. Shapiro. *Repacking Your Bags: Lighten Your Load for the Rest of Your Life*, 2nd Edition. San Francisco: Berrett-Koehler Publishers Inc., 2002.

Lucado, Max. *Cure for the Common Life: Living Life in Your Sweet Spot*. Nashville: Thomas Nelson Inc., 2005.

BOOKS BY THE INTERVIEWEES

Davidson, John. *Jesse's Journey: A Canadian Story*. Surrey, BC: Timberholme Books Ltd, 2001.

Davidson, John with Sharon Brennan. *The Right Road: How Far Will You Go?* London, ON: Binea Press Inc., 2010.

Hobson, Alan and Cecilia Hobson. *Climb Back From Cancer: A Survivor and Caregiver's Inspirational Journey*. Canmore, AB: Climb Back Inc., 2004.

Hobson, Alan. *From Everest to Enlightenment: An Adventure of the Soul*. Calgary, AB: Inner Everests Inc., 1999.

Hutchison, Katy. *Walking After Midnight: One Woman's Journey Through Murder, Justice, and Forgiveness*. Richmond, BC: Raincoast Books Ltd, 2006.

Mitchell, Jeanelle. *For the Love of Salad*. Vancouver: Whitecap Books, 2010.

Mitchell, Jeanelle. *For the Love of Soup*. Vancouver: Whitecap Books, 2002.

ABOUT THE AUTHORS

Dana Couillard is the founder of the Perception Ridge Institute, a company focused on Exploring the Power of Perception™. Dana graduated from the University of Calgary in 1976 with a Bachelor of Science degree and in 1977 with a Professional Diploma in Education. He is currently completing his Master of Arts in Human Development with Saint Mary's University of Minnesota. He is a professional educator, trainer, and certified coach with more than thirty years of expertise in the business, education, and not-for-profit sectors. He specializes in human dynamics and behaviour in the areas of perception, purpose, behavioural health, and execution.

He is a member of the International Coach Federation, the Calgary Association of Professional Coaches, the Association of Psychological Type International, and the Canadian Mental Health Association.

Currently a third-degree black belt, he is a member of the International Fudokan-Shotokan Traditional Karate Association and the International Traditional Karate Federation. Dana has been married to Brenda for twenty-five years. They have four grown children: Chuck (Shana), Erin, Jeff (Nicole), and Whitney (Kyle). ■

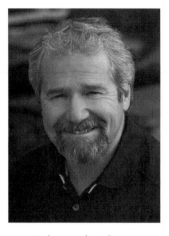

Hal Couillard has been with London Life for over thirty-six years, including seventeen years in agency management. Following his Bachelor of Commerce from the University of Calgary in 1975, he achieved the Chartered Life Underwriter, Certified Financial Planner, and Chartered Financial Consultant designations. In addition to extensive involvement in the financial services industry, Hal served eight years on the national board of Advocis, a Canadian association with approximately fifteen thousand members, representing the financial interest of millions of Canadians. During this time, he was the second youngest board chair in the over one hundred-year history of Advocis. He also served as national chair of the Chartered Life Underwriter Institute and is a charter member of the Conference for Advanced Life Underwriting. Most recently, he sat on the advisory board of the Bissett School of Management at Mount Royal University in Calgary and currently sits on the board of the Foothills Country Hospice, near Okotoks, Alberta, helping people with their final journey on Earth.

In September 2008, he and his wife, Penny, climbed Kilimanjaro in Tanzania, the highest mountain in Africa at 19,000 feet. In February 2011, he travelled to Argentina to attempt a climb of Aconcagua, at 23,000 feet the highest mountain on Earth outside of the Himalayas. He has been married to Penny for thirty-five years. They have four adult children: Chad, Brock (Erica), Adam, and Jessica.